Public Apology

Dear Beloved Readers:

If you are reading this notice, you are in possession of a re-released edition of this book. The first edit did **not** meet my standards, and should have never made it into your homes. Therefore, I had it pulled off the market, and corrected. It was very poorly edited, and full of typographical errors. I am to blame, because I rushed it to your hands. Many readers flooded my email and post office box, with letters expressing eagerness to read this book.

Finally, in an effort to keep everyone happy, I began cutting corners to speed up the process. Please accept my deepest, most sincere apology. If you own the first run of this book, please return it to our office, and I will **personally** sign, and send you a new, revised copy. I have done my very best to make sure this run is error free. If I have missed something, shoot me! I am always open to your suggestions and feedback, and I love to hear from you. I love you all. Honestly.

--Valdez

I Ain't Bitin'
My Tongue

Valdez V. Fisher, Jr.

authorHOUSE™

1663 LIBERTY DRIVE, SUITE 200
BLOOMINGTON, INDIANA 47403
(800) 839-8640
WWW.AUTHORHOUSE.COM

First published by AuthorHouse 09/19/05

ISBN: 1-4208-7458-6 (sc)

Library of Congress Control Number: 2005907600

Printed in the United States of America
Bloomington, Indiana

This book is printed on acid-free paper.

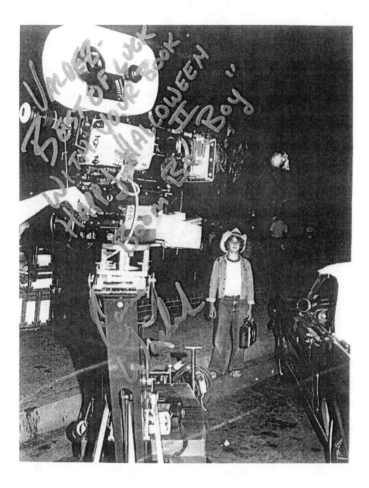

The Foreword of
Lance Warlock
Halloween II

**Not altered or edited in any way
to preserve the integrity of the submission:**

I grew up around the entertainment industry due to the fact that my father, Dick Warlock, is a 40-year veteran stuntman. My childhood was very different than most of my close friends growing up. I had the privilege of being around movie and television sets for years. I have grown up with the fact that some people see this business as a fantasy world. Not for me. It also had an effect on my brother, Billy Warlock, as he became a hard-working actor and to this day is still very strong in the business.

The bug finally bit me when I was 12 years old and was given the opportunity to play a very small, non-speaking role in the movie, Halloween II. Ironically, my father played the part of Michael Myers, the franchise's very popular mass murderer. Since that time, I have developed a love and passion for music. I have been playing drums since the age of 5, but playing seriously since age 13. Today, at age 36, I own a company called Unit 12 Productions. We compose and score music for film and television projects of all types. I am married to my junior high school love and we have 3 wonderful sons.

One day I received an email from Valdez asking me some questions about my experiences along my path in the entertainment industry. He had come across my email on my father's website. We have had an on-going friendship ever since. He has shared some of his amazing writing talents with me. His words touch your soul with kindness and truth. I don't find that in today's world, too many people are as positive as Valdez. The way he expresses himself on the pages magically transforms your attitude and your outlook. It is a privilege for me to play a small part in paving his path, as he shares with you his enlightening words. Enjoy!

-Lance Warlock

Lance Warlock Today!
Cameo Role in Halloween II
Owner of Unit 12 Productions

A Word From The Author

I would just like to take a moment to thank each of you for you readership and support. I really hope you enjoy the book. It has taken me over a year to complete this project, but the end result was worth all the hard work. I would like to pay a special tribute to the following:

<u>Cheri A. Johnson-Fisher</u>, a woman of unbelievable patience and perseverance. Thank you for being the person that you are. Plus, you make the best fried potatoes I have ever eaten.

<u>Ladonia Richardson</u>, for her patience, and talent as an ingenious graphic designer.

<u>Mitch Cohen</u>, the human dictionary, whose wisdom was called upon many times during this project.

<u>Fred W. Frank</u>, a man who fools people with a tough exterior, but has a heart of gold. God bless you, Mr. Frank.

<u>Milton Finney</u>, of the world's most feared organization. Thank you for your kindness and professionalism.

<u>James H. Brown, Sr</u>. Thank you for your many acts of kindness over the years. You were the grandpa I never had, and the nicest man I know. God bless you, Sir.

<u>J. Scott Williams</u>, a man who is never too busy to help a friend, regardless of any personal inconvenience.

<u>Gary E. Raub</u>, one of the best friends a fellow could have. A man who goes out of his way to help others, and always willing to travel the extra mile.

<u>Patricia Hawkins-Vines</u>, your wisdom is cultivating. Thank you for never being far away.

<u>Attorney Richard A. Fine</u>, thank you for helping me through one of the toughest times of my life.

<u>Attorney Andrew I. Alperstein</u>, thank you for your legal ingeniousness.

For book signings, interviews, comments or suggestions, please write:

Valdez In Print National Headquarters
Post Office Box 23951
Baltimore, Maryland 21203-5951
valdezinprint@aol.com

Again, thank you, and enjoy:

Valdez V. Fisher, Jr.

Table of Contents

Chapter 1:
I swear to tell the truth, the whole truth, and nothing but the truth...so help me, God:

All my life, I have been a creative writer, aspiring to someday write a book. Today, you hold my dream in your hands. After all the poems, love letters, and hours of online chatting, it appears I'm now *officially* an author! However, this has absolutely <u>nothing</u> to do with financial gain. I was born poor, and will probably die not far from the same. Presumably, as with **any** author, I hope my book reaches the hands of millions of readers, and seats itself on *The New York Times Bestseller List.* If it doesn't, that's quite all right too.

Perhaps I'll be invited to Oprah's talk show, **insuring** this book sells out of <u>every</u> store; or, maybe I'll just <u>give</u> all the copies away at church, and other public functions. **Whateve**r the measure of my success, there is *only* sunshine in my forecast, my friends. Why? Because I have stopped procrastinating, and fulfilled my prophecy to bring my creative penmanship to the world. Should you continue to read, you will find the title very befitting. The lines to follow depicts many of my passions and beliefs. While I cannot guarantee that you will agree with everything I have written, I can assure you that you have never, ever read anything quite like this before. If something I have written here proves to be inaccurate, I will publicly apologize. Otherwise, don't even think about asking. Be warned...I Ain't Bitin' My Tongue.

Although "dancing around the mulberry bush" does spare feelings, it also tends to compromise your foundation, when you are trying to deliver a point. This principle alone forces me to be completely forthright with you. I wholeheartedly believe this book will help people. This is the reason I have invested thousands of my own dollars, and countless hours brainstorming, to make it possible.

Before I go any further, a divine comprehension of <u>truth</u> is mandatory. **<u>Truth</u>**, is defined as: (1) the state of being the case; and (2) the body of real things, events, and facts; **<u>ACTUALITY</u>**. Now that we unequivocally understand what *truth* is <u>all</u> about, I will start with myself. Aside from a genuine, undeniable love for the craft of literary composure, I enjoy writing because I convey my thoughts so much better that way. I suffer *severely* from a panic/anxiety disorder, that makes it very difficult to speak at times. In fact, sometimes, reciting my own name, when asked, is a real challenge.

For years, I have done my very best to keep it contained. Even many who know me well, are unaware of this handicap, which has progressively worsened over the past five years. Resultantly, I have been forced to seek professional help. In the *help-seeking* process, I have attained a rather interesting education. First of all, television's portrayal of psychiatrists, doesn't even come close. TV portrays a *"shrink,"* as a soft-spoken, mind doctor, with a long leather couch for you to relax on, while discussing your troubles in their cozy, dimly lit office. No, Sir! Keep reading.

<u>*Psychiatrists*</u> are **not** *"bedside manor"* physicians. They ask you for a brief description of your problem, and medicate you in progressive dosages accordingly. Remember the old saying, "take two of these, and call me in the morning?" Well, that definitely hits the nail *square* on the head with these guys. They are like automobile mechanics, except their toolbox is a prescription pad.

Now, a <u>psychologist</u> is far different. Although not licensed to medicate, they are highly skilled troubleshooters, and extremely proficient at problem resolutions. They provide more of the imaginative atmosphere for relaxing, and venting about your woes and troubles. They listen to you attentively for thirty to forty-five minutes, and actually appear to genuinely care. However, in many instances, the concept is to keep <u>you</u> talking as much as possible.

As you ramble on, the clock continues to tick. The psychologist is well aware that it makes you feel good to vent. For this reason, most of their questions are open-ended, requiring very elaborate responses. Most who seek this form of counsel find it refreshing to have someone on their side, as the psychotherapist typically appears to be. The emotionally unstable patient appreciates a protective ally, who produces justification and rationalization for their mental upset by generally placing the blame on circumstances from their past.

For the professional, nevertheless, it's a job, and nothing more. They cannot afford to get personal. Trust me, Readers--when they go home at night, the <u>only</u> thought of you, is hoping your check clears. My intent is <u>not</u> to discount their role. For millions of people globally, these neutral confidants are a lifeline, as they do provide an outlet for voicing your cares without criticism or belittlement. When your session is up, however, they will <u>literally</u> stop you, mid-sentence. I know this for a fact, because it happened to me...more than once.

God forbid there should be some fogginess about how the therapist will get paid. If so, you'll spend the first twenty minutes of your session, hashing out deductibles and co-payments. How do I know? Take a wild guess! The most restorative and effective part of a therapeutic session, <u>always</u> appears to be at its end. Just as a patient reaches a climax of relaxation, and is most receptive, the next dollar waiting in the lobby causes him to be shut down, and shuffled out the side door.

About <u>panic</u>--I have ascertained that **even** if subconscious, it is induced by <u>fear</u>. From time to time, I ponder what *my* real fears are. Could it be the bottled up hatred, and emotional scars left from an abusive stepfather? Or, my crusade to be a good provider for my children, while depending on a volatile job market for income? Whatever the reason, something within my inner-self is very, very afraid.

For years, I have been a key officer for a large, professional corporation. I have worked very diligently to establish a reputation of reliability, trustworthiness, and competence. Resultantly, I enjoy a certain degree of job security. My role provides a significant marketing-point, not only for the company I directly represent, but a large, successful affiliate as well. It's safe to say I enjoy what I do. There is an old saying: Find a job you love, and you'll *never* **work** a day in your life. Aside from the financial rewards, the preceding decade has provided a family like work atmosphere, with a very marginal turnover.

Unfortunately, not every working class citizen shares my fondness of the workplace. Millions of people awaken daily to the dreaded chore of hammering out eight hours in an environment which they absolutely despise. People hate their jobs for various reasons. While some simply have issues with yielding themselves to authority, others complain of inadequate compensation. Still others feel they are merely insignificant pawns, on the huge corporate chess board. At workplaces across the nation, unhappy, disgruntled, discontent employees, serve at the pleasure of tyrants, whom they wouldn't afford so much as thirty-seconds notice, should they suddenly come into money, and no longer need to work.

In much of corporate America, the value of a dollar bill, outweighs the value of humanity. Some employers would even sacrifice a great working employee for an average one, if they determine it could save them a buck or two. Could these truisms induce panic? For those who answer "present" to the role call of working class America, have you ever **really** stopped to consider how great the impact of losing your job would be on your lifestyle? Loss, or even a <u>reduction</u> of income, in some instances, for as little as <u>one</u> month, can initiate the process of incinerating what has taken your entire lifetime to establish. Take your personal credit, for example.

Although to your creditors, it does not look good internally, there is <u>no</u> adverse reporting to the credit bureaus for being up to *twenty-nine* days late with a payment (automobile, credit cards, mortgage, etc.). **However**, once you hit that *thirtieth* day of delinquency, you're done! Your credit file is now black-marked, adversely affecting future interest rates on new loans, and overall future credit approval. Around the <u>second</u> month of payment delinquency, the collection calls from creditors become significantly less amicable. Few would argue that for otherwise responsible people, stumbling upon rough times is embarrassing, pride-shattering, and disheartening. However, the loss of material things, or revocation of charging privileges, is <u>far</u> from the worst of being broke.

Imagine the weight of looking into the faces of your children, knowing you have no money to feed them. Could you explain to them why strange men, <u>clearly</u> unsolicited, are removing all of the toys and furnishings from their home, and placing them on the curbside? Within me, the thought <u>alone</u> provokes panic. As a working-class individual, you are <u>always</u> vulnerable. The actions of other people can never be forecasted with 100% accuracy. Regardless how well you feel you know someone, making declarations of their capability could easily make you a liar.

It is a sad institution that in much of "Corporate America," millions work under conditions where there is clearly very little regard for them as people. Their seat beneath the "money-tree" is **100%** contingent upon their ability to perform. When unforeseen events such as extended illness, compromises or prevents their productivity, they are virtually devalued immediately. The employer's general concern is not on your misfortune, but how soon you will get back to work.

During break-room congregations beneath every sun, employers are badmouthed by their staff. They voice fruitless complaints amongst each other, ranging from the rate of pay, to the boss' unpleasant demeanor. The work itself is rarely an issue, but employee morale is easily wavered. For an employer coping with unhappy employees, the "heroic seat" can be effortlessly remounted, as often as the need to motivate arises. How? It's actually very simple: The two most effective forms of motivation in the world are <u>money</u> and <u>praise</u>. Therefore, if you aren't going to pay your people anything, at **least** take notice and appreciate the hard work they do.

The life of a poor man is infested with disadvantage. Apart from those which are obvious, the poor are generally forced to manage the random, unforeseen traumas of life, without the benefit of thoroughgoing professional help. Without question, no man, regardless of financial status, shall stand immune from life's turbulence. However, life is **not** 90% what happens, but **10%** how you react to it. Allow me to illustrate a brief comparison in a rich man's reaction to trauma, versus that of a poor man's.

When trauma strikes the life of the wealthy (stock market crash, embezzlement indictment, wrong color Mercedes was shipped, etc.), they have the wherewithal to seek as much professional counsel necessary to come to grips with their impediments, and plant their feet firmly back on life's floor. To effectively manage the more elevated levels of trauma, in-patient care may sometimes become necessary. These are called post-traumatic recovery centers (or the toilet seat of your bathroom, for poor people). At these centers, victims of upset are counseled, motivated, encouraged, coached, and commingled with other victims of upset for moral support.

A <u>poor</u> man, on the other hand, has to continue working to maintain what little he has accumulated. He has no place to run for shelter, because his money is limited. Debts are *not* forgiven because you encounter a period in which you cannot cope with life. Resultantly, a poor man, regardless of his emotional state, must continue to press towards the mark, meeting his obligations, without ever missing a beat. To a creditor, your problems are exactly that...<u>YOUR</u> problems. Although your story may be sadder than the Titanic, unless you intend to move, I suggest you get that mortgage paid.

Those who are benign enough to be born into money, are afforded the opportunity to enjoy their <u>entire</u> lives. From day one, the lifestyles that most fantasize about, is available to the "silver-spooners" as a standard. A typical working class scenario is spending the first **fifty** years of life accumulating an estate. By the time a thirty year mortgage note is divorced, and life can finally be enjoyed without the restraints of major debt, there is actually very little of life left to look forward to.

There is no *conventional* post traumatic recovery for the poor. For them, treatment is limited to prayer, keeping busy, and the ear of anyone who will listen. As aforementioned, it feels good to vent when things are troublesome... sometimes, even to a perfect stranger. Further along the subject of trauma and disorders, I have conversed with many others who suffer from panic/anxiety. To my amazement, discussions revealed disorders ranging from *performance anxiety*, (stage presentations, instrument recitals, sexual contact), to people who would **not** drive across a bridge, even if a pot of gold awaited them on the other side. Others I have met experience feelings of anxiety, simply when commingled with crowds of people. In all my comparisons, however, not **one** became paralyzed by the sound of a ringing telephone, such as I.

The initial manifestation of my disorder occurred about five years ago. When the office telephone would ring, instantly, the air would leave my lungs, and my chest would tighten. Sweat became prevalent, I would hyperventilate, and enter a state of paralysis. In many instances, I would pick up the telephone, and immediately depress the hold button, buying myself some composure time.

After a few seconds, I would raise the handset from the cradle, and attempt to speak with the caller. During the times it were my boss calling, of course, he would be thoroughly annoyed. Nonetheless, speaking sharply to a man who is having an anxiety attack does not help the situation one bit. In fact, it heightens the sensation of panic to a plateau which is virtually comparable to a heart attack. This pattern of telephone-ignited panic attacks grew increasingly consistent, and I feared losing my job as a result.

Naturally, whenever it were my boss, I would make a reasonable attempt at explaining my bizarre behavior--the telephone was not working properly, there were multiple lines ringing at once...something to that effect; <u>anything</u> except, "Sorry, Boss...when you and the customers call, it makes me really nervous. So, could you *all* just send me an email instead?"

Because the initial attacks were so fitful, denial prevented me from seeking professional help. For months at a time, the attacks would cease altogether. When they would return, however, it was with a vengeance. The increasing progression of the attacks prevented me from not being able to answer the telephone occasionally, to not being able to answer it at all. Finally, yielding to a situation that was clearly out of my control, I thought it may be very wise to have a sit-down with my employers.

<u>Communication</u>, regardless how uncomfortable or embarrassing, employs not only the assistance, but understanding of others. The disorder had matured way beyond the boundaries of concealment. Therefore, my employers needed to know that my inability to answer a ringing telephone did not stem from mere incompetence. There was a twofold reaction. While I was encouraged to *"get better,"* confusion arose as to the induction of the attacks. After nearly ten years of performing the identical tasks, what could be so frightening about a telephone?

Anxiety attacks are not only physically painful, but emotionally as well. It was extremely taxing to my pride and self esteem, having to look abnormality in the eye. A once, solo-working, decision-making veteran, had been all but reduced to clerical duties. I felt positively useless. The only hint of relief was the seldom accompaniment of coworkers, and the presence of clients in the office. As long as I were in the company of others, I felt much more at ease.

The adversities of life makes us the better for them. Also, it strengthens our stance, as we strive to encourage others who find themselves in one of life's many tough spots. Without experience, how can you possibly relate? At best, you can be an attentive listener, which **does** help. However, while a listening ear is <u>comforting</u>, the wisdom of **experience** is therapeutic. **Never**, for **any** reason, discount the value of another person's upset.

Regardless how silly, ridiculous, absurd or insignificant another person's situation sounds or appears to you--<u>unless</u> you have walked a mile in their shoes, you should <u>really</u> keep any negative commentary to yourself. For a person crawling through a low point in their life, your <u>destructive</u> benediction is **neither** appreciated **or** warranted. The problems that **you** may trample with ease, could be insurmountable to someone else. **No** college degree attainable, qualifies one man to appraise the damage to another man's emotional state, when trauma invades. Get it? Got it? Good! On the flip side, sound advice, an attentive ear, and genuine compassion often provides victims of upset with the necessary encouragement to move forward as functional human-beings.

During my bout with anxiety, my employers were very accommodating. They provided the necessary resources, monetary and otherwise, for the problem to be troubleshot, and resolved. This is the <u>difference</u> between an employer having a regard for <u>you</u>, versus a mere demand for your performance. Many people in my shoes would have been strategically fired. Cruel, eh? This is the concept of business, Readers. It happens every single day. It is <u>nothing</u> personal, so do **not** take it personally. You want the bottom line for many companies? If it <u>"ain't"</u> about **dollars**, it doesn't make **<u>sense</u>**! Understand? Great...keep reading.

Through medication, professional therapy, and writing this book, my condition has improved significantly. It is really refreshing to work for people that keep me in mind, as well as their business. In the world of business, typically your <u>performance</u> is loved...not you. Rest assured--behind <u>every</u> Christmas bonus, incremental salary increase, pep talk, board meeting, company picnic, bull roast, and pat on the back, is an indefinite agenda, geared to keeping you motivated to produce.

Just to offer yet another example of how ruthless the world of business is, when I was about eighteen years old, I worked for a small retail chain. I had only one other coworker at my location, and together we ran the shop. I was clearly the better salesman, but my coworker had more overall store knowledge. While I could sell clipped hair to a barber, he was good with the manifests, stock, and merchandising. For this reason, we complimented each other, and worked very well together.

I really enjoyed working the sales floor. I viewed <u>every</u> shopper as a buyer, and I worked very hard to sell each visitor. Another great hobby of mine during periods of down time, was looking in the stock area for old, leftover, discontinued items. I would find them, dust them off, and have them sold before lunch. Several vendors would send us sample merchandise, intended for display or promotional purposes only. Heck, I would even sell that!

At my time of hire, I *distinctly* remember being told that the <u>only</u> employee benefit, was a small percentage off store merchandise. During one of my exploratory ventures, a little over a year later, I found this not to be *entirely* true. Beneath the front wooden sales counter, well buried, and covered with ages of grime, rested a well-written employee's manual, in loose-leaf format. I cracked it open, and began to read. Inside, highlighted many key practices for managing and maintaining a profitable, organized, customer service-oriented business. Further, it discussed the company's history, and vision. But, the most intriguing tidbit of information, was after one full calendar year of service, an employee became eligible for a one week paid vacation.

Immediately, I contacted the home office, and inquired about what I had just read. They recognized the policy, honored it, and very soon thereafter, I took advantage of it. Now, my coworker had been employed there two times as long as I; and, of course, he was also interested in the newfound benefit. However, since **I** made the discovery, I was going first. It was that simple.

As soon as I returned from vacation, my coworker put his bid in. They honored his request as well, but unbeknownst to him, his vacation would be endless. While he was away, I received several in-store visits from the owner. He would poke around a bit, ask if I were okay, and scurry out the door. When my coworker returned from his vacation, I remember us standing behind the sales counter, *shooting the breeze* about how great it were to get away. We both were overjoyed that I found that binder.

A few days later, the store's owner showed up a little before quitting time. He called my coworker into the back office, and closed the door. A short time later, the door reopened, and I was advised that from that day on, I would be working the store alone. With shortage of work as an excuse, my coworker was dismissed. What I believe to have happened was, the store owner saw an opportunity to reduce that location's payroll by 50%, and acted on it.

The employer saw first hand that his business could still operate smoothly in my coworker's absence. Therefore, if I could run the store alone, and were *clearly* the better salesman anyhow, what did we need with him? You think that's cold, don't you? Well, get yourself a blanket, Reader, because the business world will <u>never</u> warm up. I told you...it's nothing personal. Are you enjoying the book so far? I hope so. Keep reading.

What's even more pathetic than millions of working-class lives, hinging upon a tyrant's mercy, is the staggering statistic of unpreparedness for a sudden loss of income. Knowing the volatility of jobs today, you should be <u>literally</u> afraid of generating unnecessary debt. Many have only a marginal amount of what they need, but nearly one-hundred percent of what they want. Finances, for scores of American families, are a juggling act. Yet, amazingly, in situations where the rent money is being applied towards the gas and electric bill, and the gas and electric money is being applied towards the automobile note, funds are still found for featherbrained spending.

Millions of people anxiously await a paycheck, that is as worthless as the stub beneath it. Where is the value in a check that was cashed and spent, before you ever saw it? A forthcoming pay on Friday, for many, means mailing off checks against insufficient funds earlier in the week, in order to keep their creditors current. What's worse, is that people have actually conditioned themselves to be comfortable with this. Across the nation, the count of those enslaved to debt continues to rise; and yet, they celebrate with more and more credit card transactions.

African-Americans, without question, are the undisputed, heavyweight, consumer champions of the world. We buy **<u>everything</u>** there is to be bought...from automobile rims that continue to spin even after the vehicle stops, to cellular telephones with navigational systems built right in. Ironically enough, I venture to say that if a door-to-door poll were conducted, many urban, African-American families, would not even have five-hundred dollars saved. I know that many people will be irritated by my summation. My intent is not to offend, but to educate and generate an awareness of very real cirumstances.

Furthermore, I am discussing the **rules**, not the <u>exceptions</u>. If you are a member of a **prominent**, urban-living, African-American family, you **are** exceptional. You have risen above statistics, and didn't retreat to the suburbs. For that, I applaud you. With retrospect, I am not from Beverly Hills **either**. I emerged from Baltimore City's lower Park Heights community, born and raised. Go there, knock on some doors, conduct your savings account poll, then see if your attitude changes. As African-Americans, we need to become increasingly determined to not only prepare for our future, but pave the way for our next generation. Instead of repeatedly winning the "*Consumer of the Year Award*," much more of our hard-earned dollars need to be routed towards investments.

Just as soldiers prepare for battle, we should prepare ourselves for unforeseen occurrences which may require access to capital. I take pride in knowing that some of the wealthiest, most educated people in America, such as William "Bill" Cosby, are people of color. However, they are also the <u>exceptions</u>. Reflecting back to urban communities, many are poverty-stricken, drug infested, and filled with youths who have been denied every possible advantage for getting ahead.

It has been a controversial observation of mine, that one of **the** more notable differences between white children, and black children, are the values. Values are a **taught** appreciation. If you as a parent, have *never* taught your child the value of financial stability, what immediate motivation does he have to work towards it? By **comparison**, white people are <u>not</u> consumers. They are investors. Is it because they are better than blacks? Not at all. The general advantage is, on a far larger scale, they are taught better economic values from day one. These values may include, the importance of a decent credit report, and the many benefits of property-ownership, versus paying rent to someone for forty years.

The more proficient you becme at manipulating a dollar bill to *your* advantage, the less likely you are to become constricted by economic challenge. It's just that simple. The **true** genesis of any caliber of success, is <u>education</u>. If Bill Gates became suddenly overcome with generosity, and randomly mailed you a check for **one million dollars**, would you **still** be a millionaire this time next year? Or, would the Mercedes-Benz manufacturer build an expansion wing in your honor, because you cleared the lots of three local retailers? Think hard. <u>Obtaining</u> wealth is comparatively simple; **retention** is where many have met with difficulty.

If you are new to money, and suddenly find yourself in possession of a lot of it, bypass the jewelry store, and drive yourself to the nearest library. Once there, read up on, and familiarize yourself with irrevocable trust funds, certificates of deposit, and other high yield investments. Each child you induct to the world should be afforded far greater advantages, than what was afforded you. This is a mark of generational progress. If you are unable to adequately and comfortably provide for a child, you should refrain from creating one. Sex is intended for the purpose of reproduction. When you reproduce irresponsibly, you play an effective role in keeping the vicious cycle of poverty alive, well, and growing.

Part of my career involves the examination of consumer credit reports. Over the past decade, in doing so, I have ascertained that many whites marry <u>young</u>, buy property <u>young</u>, and complete their education <u>young</u>. Take notice of these critical strides, while yet youthful. Education means more marketable skills, better paying jobs, and less of a likelihood of falling to poverty, or resorting to crime as a measure of survival. The unity of marriage alone generates stability. The results of two people, collectively attempting to reach goals, are far greater than that of one. Finally, the rewards of property ownership are innumerable. Additionally, it affords something of value, to be handed down to the following generation.

The reason successful blacks are so celebrated, is because, under *typical* circumstances, development-stunting obstacles are planted in our paths, almost immediately. Many African-American youths are taught by **example**, to be trendy. Particularly with youngsters, expensive clothing and automobiles are commonly viewed as a sign of wealth and accomplishment, regardless how they were obtained. It is not uncommon, in the face of poverty, for a neighborhood drug dealer, laced with gold jewelry and bulging pockets, to be viewed as a hero. We will further examine role models in a forthcoming chapter.

It has been a further observation, in my examination of credit reports, that many accounts showing delinquency, could be cleared up with less than one hundred dollars. The trouble is, so many obligors either do not care, or have never been properly educated to the value and benefits of a decent beacon score. Credit is a lot like a spare tire--you never really care about it, until you need it. Typically, it is not until credit is needed, but is not an option due to lack of credit worthiness, that people who are notorious for slow pays, and no pays, *suddenly* become interested in "making things right" with their creditors.

From a very small boy, I have wanted to achieve greatness. I have never, <u>ever</u> been content with being an "*average Joe.*" I would watch television as a child, and see how the stars live. I would drift off into deep daydreams about being rich and famous, and routinely wrote letters to local and national celebrities. At just seventeen years of age, I wrote a letter to Baltimore's **WJZ**

TV 13, declaring myself "<u>The Greatest Young Author Alive</u>." Three days later, news cameramen were setting up shop in my living room, for a live interview, before thousands of Maryland viewers! Further "shameless self-promotion" for creative writing, landed me on the front page of one of Baltimore's oldest and respected publications: the **Afro-American Newspaper.** Additionally, I was featured on the front page of the **Woodlawn Villager**, based out of Woodlawn, Maryland. More coverage of my youthful writing and motivational speaking included a radio interview on Baltimore's **Heaven 600**, a Radio One Broadcast.

Although I was the victim of a very turbulent childhood, filled with many changes and uncertainties, I now realize the many significant sacrifices my mother made for me. To a degree, it is very saddening. I love my mother more than life. Period. She has earned that. She gets on my **last** nerve three days out of the week, but I can never stay mad at her long.

Between us, there is a very marginal age difference. Resultantly, we communicate and relate very well with each other. Toys were plentiful growing up, and being the only child meant attention was never a competition. Nonetheless,

I was still somewhat lonely and subtracted. My mother wanted nothing more in life, than to give me all the things she never had growing up. Realizing this, I never pressured her for expensive clothes or tennis shoes. Up until this day, she has <u>no</u> clue the ridicule and torment I underwent, all throughout my scholastic career.

Admittedly, growing up, I was somewhat a fashion misfit. As such, I was constant ammunition for humiliation by my peers. Perhaps not *quite* this extreme, but I was the type of kid to come to school in a jogging suit, and penny loafers. Whatever was in my closet, was fine with me. Just as Jesus loved mankind enough to be teased, humiliated, and scorned, I loved my mother. I knew she was a struggling, single parent, with very little money, and I were not about to add to the problem--no matter what. I knew she wanted the best for me; so, <u>obviously</u>, she was doing her best.

I did the best I could to build a protective hedge around her. I hated anyone who ever wronged her, and wished her wrongdoers dead. She has always been a passive, genuinely sweet, trusting, easily manipulated and taken advantage of person, with a hint of a religious upbringing. For this reason, the predators of society were seemingly always close by. From abusive relationships, to prejudice coworkers, I watched helplessly as she underwent one hurt feeling, disappointment, and regret after the next.

Emotionally, for me, it was really rough at times. One day, as a young boy, I recall her pulling into a filling station, and sending me to the attendant to purchase just $1.00 worth of fuel. She had very little guidance in life, and was forced to survive basically through trial and error. At times, I think her sole motivation in life was her maternal responsibilities. She is **the** strongest, most pure woman I know.

Aside from my schoolhouse persecution, I was tormented quite a bit in my neighborhood as well. In the very early stages of my life, my mother dedicated her life to God, and was not at all shameful about it. In fact, it was not uncommon for her, with a raised window, in a Baltimore City row home, to pray and shout at the top of her lungs. This, coupled with the volume-level 50 blaring of gospel music, provided fuel for endless taunting, as scores of snickering children congregated and listened outside our small apartment.

Facing the neighborhood kids was nothing short of brutal. Routinely, I would become very angry and annoyed with my mom, for subjecting me to such ridicule. Not so long ago, as she and I shared a breakfast table, I facetiously mentioned that time in my life. She quietly responded,

"Look at them...the ones who laughed, and look at you."

I was immediately silenced by her response. There was nothing further I could possibly say. Her words to me that spring morning were profound, thought-provoking, and pregnant with truth. One of my old neighborhood buddies is currently serving a thirty, some odd year sentence for **murder** in the first degree. Another, recently staggered into my father's barbershop, high as a kite, smelling like a butt, wolfing about the shop's vending machine owing him a dollar. Unreal!

A couple summers back, as I cruised through the old "*hood,*" I noticed a girl from my past. There with her, sitting on the front porch of her house, were about ten other people--which is not *really* uncommon for Baltimore City. However, as I later learned, this was no innocent hangout. She was allowing drugs to be sold from her front steps. Now, back in the day, this girl had some of <u>the</u> toughest parents around, with very strict house rules. They were true community assets, parenting role models, and shinning examples of what our communities need so much more of. Although now both deceased, they had struggled together to pay off a thirty-year mortgage, only for their idiot daughter to reduce the property to a shipyard for cocaine. Positively unbelievable.

Today, I see life through a far broader scope, and my mother paved the way for this newfound understanding. I now realize that behind the praying, singing, shouting, whooping, and hollering, in our tiny little apartment with an open window, was simply a parent's intercession to God, to lead, guide, and protect the path of her only begotten son. Thanks, Mom! I made it. We made it!

To cap off the memory of my childhood without the forthcoming lines, would be an extreme injustice. There are some people I need to pay a very special tribute to, and acknowledge the phenomenal role they played in the foundation of my life. As far as I am aware, I really do not have a very large family. In fact, but for a few aunts, uncles, and cousins, I would have no family at all. Although my biological circle is small, we do come together at times of crisis.

One of <u>the</u> greatest advantages of family, is the benefit of collective wisdom. For this reason, those lacking a family would be at a terrible disadvanatage. However, for these people, God allocates *appointees*. These *appointees*, or "fill-in people," are called <u>extended family</u>.

When my mother was more youthful, and far less experienced, a maternal figure was sent her way. She was an older, wiser, seasoned product of a successful marriage, and the mother of three sons. She was clean, witty, firm, organized, and productive; yet, warm, loving, compassionate, and nurturing. For a time, my mother and I lived with her and her family. This was a virtual boot camp for me; a season in which the basic principals of neatness, cleanliness, and hygiene would be thoroughly reinforced. Truth is, many of the principles she instilled, I teach my own children today.

She loved, protected, and taught my mother and me. Without her, I am uncertain what would have become of us. I encourage each of you to embrace the extended family in your life. With an open heart and mind to receive, sometimes you will surely find that a friend <u>can</u> truly stand closer than a brother.

As previously written, this *Godsend* of a person had three boys; and, as a child, I was closest to her younger son. I really looked up to him. He was older than me and, well dressed, with lots of gold jewelry. He was also just an *all around*, nice guy, who was loved and respected in the neighborhood. But, as time progressed, I grew closer to the middle son.

Initially, I couldn't stand him (the middle boy) at all. In fact, I thought he was a complete jerk. He was *extremely* playful, and I was constantly the solo contestant on his game-show of pranks. One winter, I recall him throwing a snowball at me, <u>inside</u> of the house! There was also this rib punch he would do to me, that immediately knocked all the wind from my body. I would fall to the floor, gasping for air, like a trout out of water.

Another painful recollection, was a time he came to my mother's apartment to baby-sit me. One Friday night, he lifted me repeatedly above his head, tossed me upwards, and then caught me, as I "*weeeeeeeeed*" with delight! This action continued several moments, until he got the unprovoked, malefic urge to throw me <u>outward</u> this time, instead of upward. I flew out about five feet, and landed flat on my face, to the solid tiled floor. As I laid there crying, I could hear his sinister snickers of satisfaction behind me, as my agony served as sort of a macabre entertainment for him.

Of course, I had no idea how close we would eventually become. Today, he is my very best friend in the whole world. Throughout my teenage years, he looked out for me. He was the big brother and confidant I never had, but desperately needed. He made sure I had money and food. He also made his protective presence known to my abusive, psychotic stepfather, whom I feared.

On Friday evenings, he would come to pick me up in his little black sports car, armed with an array of jokes to tell, and a whole weekend to get them told. It is safe to say, the zenith of my life, at that particular stage, was spending weekends with him. In my opinion, the good he has done for me and others, atones him for any bad he could ever do. Until this day, he remains a true comic--one laugh after another. Going to the movies, shooting pool, or shopping for groceries at the supermarket...whatever the happening, his presence <u>alone</u> sensationalizes the event.

As if it were yesterday, I remember sitting in my high school classroom, totally disinterested in what the teacher had to say. My total concernment was Friday afternoon! In so many instances, I really do not know what I would have done without him. He was my hero, my brother, and my friend. Thank you, Donald.

I respectfully dedicate this chapter to the Grant Family.

Chapter 2:
The Commentary

The amazing thing with <u>success</u> is, even the people who can't **stand** you as a person, are forced to respect your position in life. Take Donald Trump, for example. I personally think he's a genius, but not everyone shares my appreciation. If I were in his shoes, I would do many of the same things. In concert with hosting reality television shows, and plastering my name all over buildings, I would sail the seas in my yacht, docking at random shores to hobnob with the commoners.

I would give generously to the poor, and provide orphanages, nationwide, with toys, clothing, food, and monetary resources. Desiring to never lose touch with my foundation, I would routinely return to the place it all began, Baltimore City, to set up and fund social programs. Never would I become too important to shake a hand, or lecture at a high school. If **only** I had the money, as Mr. Trump does, to bring my dreams to reality, my superstardom would be notably unconventional.

Donald J. Trump, aside from being my personal role model, is a known strategist and astute business man, with a faculty for making the **right** move, at the precise time. Just to look at him--that smirk of wealth, power, and accomplishment, makes it abundantly apparent that he is absolutely in love with himself. I think that's fantastic. Your <u>first</u> love affair should begin with the person you see in the mirror. If you do not love yourself, any love you have for anyone else is dysfunctional. One day, I logged onto America Online, and noticed a solicitation for the new <u>Donald Trump, Platinum Visa Card</u>! You <u>GO</u> boy! Unbelievable! Ever since I were a teenager, I have written unanswered letters of admiration to him.

In 1994, however, he did autograph my copy of his book, "Trump...The Art of the Deal." I sent it to his office, along with instructions for a mile long benediction. What I received back was, "Best Wishes--Donald Trump." Not <u>exactly</u> what I asked for, Buddy! As with most people, his signature bares no resemblance to his actual name, whatsoever. His last name appeared to have about sixteen U's in it...*Truuuuuuuuuuuuump*.

About five years ago, I took my two small daughters to Manhattan, New York. Believe it or not, we were on a *Home Alone II, Lost in New York*, movie quest. I took my children to F. A. O. Swartz, which in the movie was *Duncan's Toy Chest*. We went to the suite used by actor *McCaulay Culkin* in the film, at the luxurious, world renowned, **Plaza Hotel**, and visited Central Park.

We even reenacted the chase scene, wherein *McCaulay* ran to the hotel's concierge, pleading for protection from the pursuing bandits. As I stood beneath the Plaza's canopy, and my children ran to me for help, I asked, "What's the matter... store wouldn't take your *STOLEN* credit card? Let's see what the police have to say about this!" By the way...unless recently installed, the Plaza Hotel does **not** have a swimming pool, as the movie suggests. That scene was shot elsewhere.

The zenith of my children's New York City experience, was a toss-up between actually visiting the Plaza Hotel, a place they clearly recognized from the movie, and physically shopping for toys at what they knew as Duncan's Toy Chest. For me, however, the building to the immediate left of the toy store, was the ultimate attraction; it was the **Trump Tower.** After leaving the store, we next visited the tower. From the second I stepped foot inside, I unequivocally realized that there is so much more to life than work and traffic jams. Could you imagine having one of the most prestigious New York City structures, named after you? I have so much respect and admiration for Mr. Trump, that if he had walked by, which assumably was a real possibility, I am not sure what I would have said to him.

I remember scrolling the rolodex of executives and businesses occupying the tower. I scanned thoroughly for Mr. Trump's name, but it was not there. At this point, I was uncertain if he actually maintained an office there, or if the tower were merely another investment. As aforementioned, many have mixed feelings about "The Donald." His name alone invokes commentary, ranging from his development of first-class structures and casinos, to his purported Masters Degree in womanizing.

My elevated interest in Mr. Trump compels me to read all I can, and watch as many television broadcasts available, with his regard. In what I have seen and read, it is not uncommon for commentators to deliver kidney punches about his marriages, skillful business bankruptcies, and vivacious spending habits. However, I've **yet** to notice *anyone* deny his knack for effective performance, under extreme pressure. Quite the contrary, as the media reports, he has strategically risen from the brink of **personal** bankruptcy, to regain his seat at the table of American <u>Billionaires</u>. Try logging on to www.get-outta-debt.com, and accomplish the same feat.

Shifting slightly to another direction, success is mocked quite a bit also. As people cruise the streets in expensive automobiles, there is an automatic presumption of financial stability. First of all, the world's most <u>unreliable</u> gage of a man's wealth, is what he drives. Nowadays, anyone with a pulse can acquire a vehicle loan. Society has conditioned us to believe "the more flash, the more cash." The truth is, some people are "**all** show, and **<u>no</u>** dough!" In short, things are <u>not</u> always as they appear.

Furthermore, money is not the only measure of wealth. **Wealth**, the word itself, is widely misconceived. Wealth, merely means surplus. You can have a wealth of many things, including misery. Some of the wealthiest people on the face of the earth, do not have so much as two nickels to rub together. Without a **wealth** of happiness and self-contentment--even for the Bill Gates' of the world, you are dirt poor. All the yachts, private islands, beautiful women and billionaire status in the world, will not help a distraught man to sleep at night.

There is no standardized measure of success, as it equates to different things, for different people. For some, success could be the mere obtainment of a high school diploma. Others may have aspired to drive a Mercedes-Benz all their lives, and finances finally permits. Personally, at this juncture, effective parenting is the single greatest plateau of success I could possibly reach. I take an enormous amount of pride in fathering my children, and setting a standard in their lives.

What children need, even <u>more</u> than **financial** support, is the basic application of <u>yourself</u>, as a parent. Thousands of children benefit from adequate finances, but are still victims of neglect. How is this possible? Here are a few examples:

1. If your children have been telling you for the past three hours that they are hungry; yet, you cannot log out of an online chat room long enough to tend to them, you are guilty of neglect.

2. If <u>you</u> walk around, looking like you've just leaped from a GQ centerfold; while behind you, drags your crying, unhappy, snot-nosed kid, with an ice-cream stained

shirt, and dried food residue all over his face, you are guilty of neglect.

3. If your child tells you they aren't feeling well; and, rather than investigate thoroughly, you just shuffle them off to school, you are guilty of neglect.

4. If you are an able-bodied man; yet, your kid is calling **another** man Daddy, because that <u>other</u> man is fulfilling your parental role, you are guilty of neglect.

5. If due to your repeated broken promises or procrastination, your child cannot rest on your word as a parent, you are guilty of neglect.

6. If this book is so captivating, that you can't put it down to help with your child's homework, you are guilty of neglect.

7. If the first day of school is September 3; is it now June 5, and your child's teacher has **<u>no</u>** clue what you look like, you are guilty of neglect.

Children have absolutely <u>zero</u> say in who parents them. They are helpless, defenseless little creatures who are born to this world deserving of love, nurturing, support, patience, and protection. In addition to being afforded no parental consideration, they have no control of their environment, or whom they come into contact. For this reason, you have an absolute responsibility to keep any child in your charge, safe, sheltered, and in an environment which will preserve and promote their physical and mental well-being.

Now, let's elaborate on <u>role models</u>. When people make mention of *role models*, the typical reference is of positive people. **However**, a role model is <u>not</u> necessarily a person of positive influence. A role model is <u>merely</u> someone who you admire, and are motivated by. They can range from Donald Trump, to a neighborhood street thug. Therefore, when we fail to saturate our children with **positive** role models, we leave a vacant, available seat for **negative** ones.

These negative influences could be the partial blame for poor choices, potentially altering the course of your child's entire life. A child, raised in an environment where the greatest person to be looked up to is a drug addict, increases his likelihood of drug experimentation by at <u>least</u> 50%. How far you excel in life is dependent upon your level of drive, determination, and motivation. When motivation is low or absent, so is the drive to press towards the mark of noteworthiness.

At least for me, my father has always been a positive role model. Although he was no angel by **any** stretch of the imagination, he was particularly cautious about his children's intake of negativity. As a child, he would **never** take me to see horror films, although they were my favorite. Truth is, in thirty-one years, I have <u>never</u> heard my father curse, seen him smoke, drink alcohol, fight, or disrespect anyone. Today, he remains a well groomed, attractive, financially stable, community icon, who has emerged from the ashes of typical, low-income, "neighborhood living."

He is a brilliant businessman, and well disciplined. He makes his opposition of frivolous spending known, and his ever-climbing success makes it very difficult to refute his benediction. He is not only in business locally, but has ventured into the profitable world of investment real estate, routinely purchasing properties of a substantial cost, with straight cash.

Despite the occasional "*bump-in-the-road*" in our father/son relationship, I have always respected his opinion. Reflecting back to the opening statement of this chapter; you have **no** choice but to respect the position of a man, given no real *head start* by way of inheritance, lottery jackpot winning, trust fund, "good neighborhood," or formal education; who has fathered six children, gone into business for himself, and acquired the wherewithal to retire slightly after forty. Many of us work jobs we detest for fifty years, to receive a cheesy, gold-plated wrist watch, and an insufficient retirement check.

Of all the influences a child encounters, **parental** influence is the most penetrating. Dionne and I share two little girls...Sammy and Rosalind. Since they were babies, I have worked for the same company, and rarely missed time. I wanted them to see, particularly as females, that a **real man** goes to work everyday, and provides for his family. I have fought very hard to be a rock for them, and accustom them to at least a middle-class lifestyle. We have an excellent father/daughter relationship, and I sensationalize each and every one of their accomplishments. Arguably, I give them a little too much, but I justify it with their exceptional scholastic performance. In all honesty, the breakup of their Mom and I severely compromised their happiness, and much of what I do for them is compensatory.

Dionne was an emotional wreck during and after our fall-apart. Our marriage of five years had crumbled, and her only therapy was to distance herself. During this time, it would just be me and the girls. I stepped up to the plate as a father, more so than ever before. I had <u>no</u> social life whatsoever, but I was where I were needed most--in position, raising my children. In the midst of all the turmoil, I was determined to provide some semblance of stability. For all involved, I knew the days to come would get a lot worse, before they get better. I bonded with my children, and <u>only</u> left their side to go to work. In the lyrics of Gospel Singer **CeCe Winans**, "It wasn't easy, but it was worth it!"

Without question, children are wondrous creatures. They are cute and energetic, with mouths that can outrun diesel engines. Some of the world's most humorous and fascinating things are said by kids. Referring back to my daughter's love for the movie Home Alone II, Lost in New York, there is a scene wherein Kevin, (McCaulay Culkin), is solicited by some hookers to "read him a bedtime story." In the movie, hookers are portrayed as beautiful, erotic dream girls.

One day, I picked Rosalind up from school. She must have been five years old at the time.

At dismissal, many of the teachers assumed a hall monitoring detail, ensuring that each child moved along without incident, and advanced to the appropriate exit. As we passed by one of the teachers that Rosalind recognized, she stopped, looked at her, and said, "Daddy! She's beautiful. She looks <u>just</u> like a **hooker lady**!" All I could do was smile, pull Rosalind down the hall, and leave the building as quick as possible. That was just one of life's little embarrassing moments that you wish you could erase; but, in Rosalind's pure little innocent heart, her comment were <u>the</u> greatest of compliments.

Rosalind, for the most part, is a very angry child. She is outspoken, and highly territorial. She is excessively protective of those she loves, and makes her lack of love abundantly apparent to those she dislikes. She displays a very limited regard for consequence. She is a lazy child who avoids leaving the house, and enjoys napping as often as possible. She is unusually intelligent, and speaks with wisdom and sarcasm, far beyond her years.

Rosalind is <u>very</u> organized, in a highly **unconventional** way. Her bedroom is usually trashed. The bed itself, has enough toys on it to fill a chest, and the type of toys she asks for would give most kids the willies; everything from snakes, to lizards, spiders and frogs. However, even in the midst of that catastrophe of a sleeping quarter, **every** single toy is strategically placed, precisely where she wants it. If you bother **any** <u>one</u> of them, even in her absence, she will know immediately upon her inspection, and angrily address your meddling.

You want Rosalind for a playmate? Fine. Here are the rules: She is in charge, and she's the boss. The <u>only</u> opinion that matters is hers, and you **will** do things her way. You will not speak a treasonable word against her, her laws, or loved-ones. You have a problem with that? Fine, again. Get out of her room; <u>all</u> the way out. Remove <u>everything</u> you came with; otherwise, it **will** be removed for you. Also, you'd better hope there is an adult nearby to oversee the eviction; otherwise, you'll receive a pinch, or something painful as you're leaving. Sometimes, even an adult's presence will not safeguard you against whatever she feels is your punishment for disobedience.

Now, would you like to get back into Rosalind's good grace? OK. Heres what needs to be done: First, confess and repent for your *sins*. In this case, <u>*sin*</u> is defined as **whatever** you did to piss her off. This ceremony of apology continues as long as Rosalind deems it necessary...usually several minutes. Next, you'd better **really** mean what you're saying. In fact, she'll insist that you actually declare sincerity. Finally, you will sit, touch only what you are permitted to touch, and obey her aforementioned commands. Do this, and you'll have a friend for life.

A few years back, I was driving down the road, when Rosalind decided she wanted a McDonald's chicken sandwich for lunch. I made a parental decision that we were eating at home this day, and she got extra perturbed. She grabbed my right hand, raised it up to her mouth, and bit down into my flesh with all her might. The pain was so excruciating, that I had to pull over to compose myself. As cute as she is, I remind her constantly that she's not too cute for a spanking.

Sammie is Rosalind's older sister, and Dionne was undergoing a lot of emotional trauma while pregnant with her. She routinely felt sad, alone, and discouraged. At then age eighteen, she felt trapped, and terribly intimidated by her forthcoming responsibilities. I comforted and encouraged Dionne as often as I noticed the need, reassuring her that she would soon give birth to a beautiful, healthy baby.

Aside from a huge stomach, the pregnancy induced severe acne, and her face had swollen to the size of a tractor wheel. This new, *pregnant* appearance, contributed significantly to her depression. In my eyes, however, she were just as beautiful as always. When I looked at her, all I saw was a girl I had loved since I were a kid. Even if an eye developed in the center of her forehead; to me, she would have been the cutest cyclops in the world. I loved her unconditionally.

Before I advance in this story, I would like to briefly explain unconditional love. Loving someone **unconditionally**, means that your love is **<u>not</u>** compromised by their shortcomings, weaknesses, mistakes or inadequacies.

May 5, 1993, Sammie was born. She was an exceptionally large baby, with cheeks that looked like she had apples inside. They sorta hung downwards, like the Tweety Bird's. When she smiled, her little mouth revealed pure gum-line; and, her slightly slanted eyes were ammunition for endless Chinese jokes. She was the cutest baby many had ever seen.

As she grew, Sammie became quite a trend setter too. Many of her "baby-sayings" are still facetiously used in family conversations today.

Few who know her would deny, the most classic of her saying was "Shut up, **<u>OING</u>**!" Many children between the ages of two and four, undergo what I call the "shut up and bite stage." Sammie was notorious for both.

I, for one, routinely fell victim to Sammie's teeth. Scores of others were commanded by her to shut up, oing! What she was intending to say was, "Shut up, <u>*all right.*</u>" However, since she couldn't pronounce *all right*, it came out <u>*oing.*</u> We would all roar with laughter. Today, Dionne and I tell each other all the time, shut up, oing! Occasionally, even now at age twelve, Sammie will still hit you with it.

Sammie's thighs bulged with baby-fat. By age one, she looked to be about forty pounds. By comparison, Sammie was the lost child of a giant. One of her very first words was eat, and it echoed from her crib regularly. To her, <u>every</u> baby was a Sammie. After Rosalind were born, Sammie would tell Dionne and I all the time, that **Sammie** (Rosalind) was crying.

Sammie was a legendary baby, who's mere presence drew attention, where ever she was taken. One day, at the supermarket, an elderly woman took one look at Sammie, and told her,

"I love you." Another time, the playful Sammie dashed from our apartment, into the neighbor's open apartment door across the hall. Incidentally, she was a Chinese lady. The lady picked Sammie up, looked at Dionne and me, and cried, "<u>MY</u> baby!"

Dionne's grandfather was driving along one day, as Sammie played in the back-seat of his car. Suddenly, the back of his head became a snack, when she decided to bite it. Another time, she bit me too. When I asked why, she explained that I was a cheese-steak! From her earliest stages of life, she has been an exceptionally bright, happy, helpful, meticulous child. How meticulous is she? Sammie is the kind of kid who stands her glass beside her sister's, to make certain they have equal amounts of orange juice.

She loves complicated gadgets, and is proficient at assembling things which seem to come in a thousand pieces. She is an extremely sore loser, and <u>must</u> win at **every** game she plays. When she does not, she becomes immensely disheartened and frustrated. Occasionally, she will even cry. Her superior dedication to scholastic achievement, routinely lands her on the highest academic list known to the Maryland public school system: <u>The Principal's Achievers</u>.

Sammie has excelled scholastically since the day she stepped foot into a classroom. Her "book-wormish" traits assures teacher's pet status, each and every school year. She is noticeably discontent to receive **anything** other than what she asks for. If chocolate cake is the request, you could cut the ungratefulness with a knife if you bring home doughnuts instead. Sammie is very cowardly at times, and Dionne's position as a disciplinarian seems to intimidate her, a heck of a lot more than Rosalind.

Without question, the bulk of the arguments between Dionne and me, had stemmed from the children. As I mature parentally, I strive to grant more consideration to Dionne's points of view. Not all of what she says is wrong; with retrospect, not everything I say is right. As a father, I want my children to grow up slow. As aforementioned, I believe firmly that each person with a child in their charge, is duty-bound to provide a better life for that child, than what was provided for them.

This is evidence of generational progress. Growing up, having **either** of my parents at my schoolhouse meant I were in serious trouble. For millions of parents, every scheduled hour of work is detrimental to their economic welfare.

Resultantly, their equally important role as chief overseers of their child's academic development, takes an unfortunate back-seat to finances. No matter what the circumstance; when you are removed from the equation of your child's scholastic career, you compromise the quality of their education.

As a parent, you cannot expect a teacher to take a personal interest in your child, when seemingly, you have not even taken one yourself. The children of parents who make their supportive presence known, are educated better than those who do not. Trust me. In addition, it boosts your child's confidence, morale, and self esteem, to look into the audience from a school stage, and see your face. Faculty and students alike, are **<u>forced</u>** to respect the child of a parent who is <u>never</u> far away.

Personally, I feel that Dionne allocates the girls far too much responsibility, for their ages. At the same time, her claim is that I baby them excessively, and refuse to let them grow up. Who's right? Who's wrong? Who knows? What can be agreed upon, however, is the major variances in our parenting techniques.

Dionne takes the warden approach. She is very stern, and often closed-minded to the children's opinions. With regard to toys, and other unwarranted rewards, she is not particularly gratuitous. Dionne's take is that, aside from the bare necessities, extras should be earned, not given. For the girls, a good report card is the best chance of shopping for something other than clothes.

In concert with the obvious benefits of <u>two</u> active parents, comes a much needed balance. While Dionne feels rewards are strictly for accomplishments, I routinely take the girls on elaborate shopping sprees, even when their behavior has been less than perfect. My biggest overall concern with their mother/daughter relationship, is the potential communication deficiency. I warn Dionne constantly, that coming off as too much of a "hard nose," induces the concealment of what could be very fundamental issues. On the contrary, when your children feel comfortable that they will not be ridiculed when confiding in you, they are more apt to be forthcoming, truthful, and candid. Based on the tempo of the current day, this is **precisely** the relationship you should <u>pray</u> to have with your children.

Particularly nowadays, you need to have the first shot at addressing the concerns of your children. Otherwise, that call for guidance could default to some outsider, who may not only provide detrimental advise, but manipulate your child's vulnerability to their advantage. Many parents routinely assume the role of a prosecuting attorney, when their children voice concerns. While you may not agree with everything your children say or feel, listen to them carefully. Try not to make every conversation with you an uphill battle for them. This is very frustrating for a child, and you will find yourself being furnished critical information, only after a situation has expanded way out of control.

Without question, thousands of children are sent to school each day with a depreciated capacity for learning. Why? Because they genuinely did not feel their best, and need to have been loved and nursed at home. Yes, children **do**, on occasion, have the tendency to stage illness, in order to be off from school for a day. Nonetheless, parental discernment is not always an effective detector of truthfulness. This is not to say that your intelligence should be insulted either. Sometimes, fakers are blatantly obvious. During the times you just aren't sure, don't chance it. Let them stay at home, but try these tactful methods of dealing with your <u>sick</u> child.

<u>First</u> of all, a sick day is **not** a leisure day; nor should it be treated as such. **Sick** people need bed rest, and <u>lots</u> of it. This means, for the **entire** day missed, and each day missed thereafter, there should be **no** Play Station II, television watching, outdoor playing, Internet access, comic books, Game Boy Advance, doodle pads, compact discs, or <u>anything</u> else *entertaining*. The child should be treated lovingly, and nursed back to health. However, a clear message should be sent that **sick** people need relaxation, not amusement. This message reinforces itself after school, as the sound of playing children can be heard from your child's bedroom window. The revocation of all the things that makes being a kid fun, assures a very boring day. I promise you...your child will think twice before staging illness again.

Effective parenting is a gentle blend of guidance, compassion and friendship. For a child today, there is an overwhelming amount of adversity. As a parent, you will not have the answer to every question, so do not feel inadequate. On occasion, your child may illustrate disturbing behavior, which will leave you befuddled. A key ingredient of your parental role is your acknowledgment of where your ability ends, and the professionals' begin. Many parents are reluctant to seek professional help for their children, because in doing do, they face the potential revelation that their child is abnormal.

As parents, you need to remain cognizant that <u>mental</u> health is <u>just</u> as front-page as <u>physical</u> health. Emotional upset sometimes requires superior craftsmanship and tact to sever the root. As aforementioned, although professional counselors do not get personally involved, they provide a neutral outlet to express concerns, in a secure environment. For millions, this is where healing begins. Sometimes, the psychological baggage from breaks-up, death, or divorce, just to offer examples, rest dormant for years. Meanwhile, subconsciously, our mental health steadily deteriorates, as the ladle of life dumps even more of life's perils into our bowls.

As perhaps you've noticed, I have a vivid recollection of my childhood. Many of the occurrences which I store in memory, are disremembered to others who partook in them. They listen in astonishment, as I recount in graphic detail, events which for them are very sketchy at best. However, the laughter of reminiscing, suddenly comes to a chilling, attentive silence, when I make mention of my childhood gift of dreams and visions. The supernatural realm is an avenue that thoroughly mystifies even the most adamant believers. As a child, through clear, decisive dreams and visions, I became forewarned of events to come.

My great grandfather and I were very close when I was a small child. Every place he went, I cried to come along. I had the run of his house, and were seldom denied anything I asked for. I drank from a baby's bottle until I were nearly five years old. On more than one occasion, on my own accord, I concluded I was too old for it, and insisted it be thrown away. Each time I made this declaration, it resulted in him sending his wife to the convenience store, in the middle of the night, to replace it.

We all called my grandfather, Papa. I can still see him smiling at me, as I would kneel down alongside his bed most nights, and say my goodnight prayers. I brought life to him, and anyone who upset me in his presence, felt his wrath. Papa had a little, fire-engine red, gasoline lawnmower. I still remember him cranking it up for me, because I thought it was exciting to hear it run.

Most mornings, his wife would make eggs for me, and turn on what she called *the film funnies* (cartoons). One night, as Papa and I laid in bed, I kept licking his arm, and laughing at his frustration with it. After about the fifth warning to keep my tongue in my mouth, he slowly reached on the night stand for a small belt, and placed it underneath the blankets. The very next time I attempted to lick him, my tongue was greeted with a swift lash of belt leather.

One evening, after reciting my nightly prayer, still knelt on the carpeted floor, I sadly looked up at him, and told him he was going to die. A vision told me so. With a confused look, he refuted my claim, and assured me he would not. He told me not to worry. Less than one year later, I remember touching his hardened face, begging him to awaken, as his lifeless body laid inside a half-opened coffin. At then age five, the pain of losing him was absolutely unbearable.

The sorrowful days and nights to come would number many. The theme song from the television show "Taxi," reminded me of him, and often made me cry. I held on to the fantasy that he would return, and I would awaken from an awful dream. My parents were in no way equipped to manage the psychological trauma I underwent, and would continue to undergo for years, after Popa's death. Resultantly, for a good portion of my youth, I wrestled with a submerged, recurring depression.

Evidence of a still open wound, surfaced the day my father and I visited Papa's grave site. I was five years old when he died, and at least fifteen when my dad and I made the visit. I pleaded with my father not to take me there, but he was insistent. I stood atop the grave, paralyzed by grief, sorrow, and fond childhood memories of him. When we left the cemetery, I was upset and withdrawn for the next hour or so.

The next significant occurrence was when I were eighteen years old. I was lying quietly on my living room floor, and began to cry uncontrollably, as I reflected back on my experiences with Papa, and the immeasurable bewilderment I felt after his death. I could still image his lifeless body laying there, non-respondent to my cries for him. I felt as if I were being stabbed in the heart with a dagger, all over again. Although we have only the best intentions in our efforts to comfort victims of traumatic upset, the effectiveness of our counsel is very limited, as nonprofessionals. In the management of any magnitude of emotional trauma, it is always advisable, if possible, to consult with a professional. Do not be ashamed. The end result will be a far healthier mind, body, and soul.

Chapter 3:
Disaster Strikes

The many curve-balls of a lifetime can make your **worst** nightmare, a devastating reality. Who would have thunk, in a *million* years, I would break up with Dionne? While a student of the **Garrison Middle School**, in Baltimore City, there was a particular schoolmate whom I noticed, but never really paid much attention. She was tall and slender...sorta like *Olive Oil*, (Popeye's animated wife.) Of all the times I had seen her in passing, never had we exchanged two words until one cool spring afternoon, in 1989, when the day's classes were canceled for a school-wide cookout.

After spotting her on the playground, standing beside a fence, I walked over to her, and we began to talk. It would **definitely** be safe to say, I liked Dionne immediately. There was just something about her that, until this very day, I cannot quite place my finger on. I gave her my telephone number, and she soon called. Our conversations were timeless. Many hours a day we would spend with telephone receivers glued to our ears. Occasionally, we would even fall asleep, mid-conversation. Admittedly, my feelings for

Dionne rapidly matured from a "*deep like*," to a borderline obsession.

As if it were yesterday, I recall visiting Dionne at home for the very first time. It was *storybook* romance; I had walked for miles in a downpour of rain, and was dripping wet when I arrived at her doorstep. Seeing her outside of a school setting was truly a rediscovery. I had never realized how attractive she really was. Since I were primarily disinterested in school anyway, to me, all the students and staff looked the same. I remember kissing her for the first time that day, and knowing <u>without</u> question, I was absolutely in love with her.

During this time, although a tremendous tease, Dionne was yet a virgin. Sex for her, at that avenue in her life, was positively out of the question. Many nights, I would leave her apartment, *hot and bothered*, with an erection that could hail a taxi. When Dionne and I were not together, she was on my mind; and, the mere thought of her provoked impulsiveness. I sent her cards regularly, and were known to call, just to tell her I loved her. I did love Dionne as much as a teenaged boy knew how to love; but, befuddling enough, we were never *officially* in a committed relationship until several years later. Nonetheless, she were the apple of my eye.

Although spending time with Dionne was more exhilarating than <u>any</u> thrill ride, I would routinely become very irritated by the nonexistence of sexual intimacy with her. It is my belief that love is a progressional embarkment. It reaches higher and higher plateaus, ultimately resulting in the institution of marriage. Even afterwards, it should remain ceilingless as it's rudimentary principals are rediscovered, and put into demonstration, time and again. Because Dionne was not ready for intimacy, I felt our love was at a progressional standstill. For this reason, I would periodically become overtaken with frustration, and not speak to her for months at a time. Although repeatedly vowing not to, I always found my way back to her life.

In 1993, Dionne and I finally shared that magical evening. I remember thinking it was a dream. I knew she would become my wife someday, but were uncertain of the play-by-play events to come. Many search their whole lives for their "soul mate." When he/she arrives, you will know, without question. It actually requires very little action on your part. Since the second Dionne and I connected, I was mesmerized by her. In

1994, she went on record as my girlfriend. Her respect for, and commitment to our relationship became immediately apparent. I did not feel the slightest bit of insecurity.

On a freeze-frame, life could **not** have been more perfect. I had the girl of my dreams, a little job, and a brand new car on top of it all. An addict's high on cocaine, was no comparison to my high on life. The amazing thing about life, however, is that one day you can feel on top of the world; the next day, it can feel the world is on top of <u>you</u>. In the sequence of events to follow, the only anchor in my life, was my relationship with Dionne. First, after a disagreement with management, I made the *ingenious* decision to walk off my job. Less than a month later, I entered the path of a speeding motorist, and pulverized my car.

A short time later, Dionne became pregnant, and moved in with me. She was often very emotional, temperamental, and frustrated about her pregnancy. She cried a lot, and routinely expressed insecurity. I can only imagine that being pregnant by an unemployed man, without the benefit of marriage, <u>would</u> induce recurring feelings of uncertainty. At times, nothing seemed to make her happy.

During this time, Dionne and I argued a great deal. At bedtime, if I were angry with her, I exercised a very abusive habit of turning my back to her in bed. Let's very quickly examine the three most **common** forms of abuse:

1. **Physical**--actual harmful contact

2. **Verbal**--malevolent commentary

3. **Psychological**--silent treatment, distant behavior, seclusion

One night, after a heated debate, I turned my back to her in bed, huffed with frustration, and closed my eyes. Fed up with my childishness, she grabbed my arm with the strength of an animal, and rolled me completely back around to face her. From that night, I nicknamed her "Bear Lady;"in accordance, I became "Bear Man;" and obviously, our apartment was our cave.

These days were pregnant with the fundaments in which true relationships are built. Although we had little else, there was an abundance of love. Even when life had beat me down to bent knee, Dionne's trust and belief in me never wavered. I stood as a man, and never let my petrification shine through. I was under an enormous amount of pressure, and afraid of failure. I was without a car, job, or plan.

Morning after morning, I would leave the cave, riding buses from one fruitless job interview to another. Most of the time, I couldn't even afford to eat lunch. Many would agree, at least from a working class perspective, the employment market is a real joke. A help wanted sign exists to decorate the door. In 1995, I got the break I had been praying for. I became employed by "Bear-Haul" (U-haul), and was making a substantial amount of money.

Later the same year, I married Dionne in a church ceremony, and was promoted to management on my job. Life again, was simply fantastic. When I would come home, sometimes from a thirteen hour shift, Dionne would literally jump up and down cheering, "Bear Man is home to the cave...YAY!" If **only** I had realized how precious that was. Around this time, Dionne and I enjoyed a middle-class lifestyle. We dined out, and participated in recreational events constantly, sparing no expense in doing so. When my cash ran thin, I demonstrated no reluctancy in pulling out a charge plate.

My prodigious spending habits soon landed the Bear Family in serious financial trouble. We were already up to our necks in debt; and yet, I just kept spending, as if anticipating a multimillion dollar inheritance. From a motorcycle, to a Mercedes Benz, and frequent trips to Atlantic City, I lived the life of Warren Buffet's grandson. Before long, but for a revolving line of credit, we would have been paupers.

Dionne's grandfather and I became very close friends. He admired and appreciated the outstanding job I <u>appeared</u> to be doing at taking care of his granddaughter. He was retired, financially stable, and a very strong pecuniary resource. From him, I borrowed tens of thousands of dollars, in an attempt to overcome a massive deficit, and reclaim financial stability. Ironically, during these days, Dionne didn't work, nor did I want her to. I wanted to stand up, and be a man. The mere suggestion of sending my wife to some order-barking dictator, was a rebate to my manhood.

Working overtime was no longer optional. If I were to sustain in my financial traffic jam, it was essential that I earn a certain amount of money each pay. People in this position are **slaves**. Being a <u>slave</u> to debt, is a <u>slave</u> nonetheless. As if my back was not already making an indentation in the wall, the stress affected my job performance, and I found myself unemployed yet again.

It took no time flat for my entire financial world to crumble. I owed thousands of dollars to the banks, my car and credit card payments were way behind, and the collection calls were a brutal progression from friendly reminders, to threats of litigation. The pressure was unbelievable, to the point of even affecting my marriage. At times, I literally felt like my head was going to explode. I actually had to call the local telephone company, and order the Caller ID feature, so I would know when it was safe to answer the telephone.

In 1997, acting on my father's recommendation, I enrolled in college to gain the necessary skills to enter the field in which I continue to work today. However, the initial, entry-level position did not exactly land me on the cover of Forbes. Meanwhile, my credit situation continued to suffer. One night after dinner, as Dionne and I arrived at the cave, I spotted a suspicious looking, gray colored panel van in the parking lot of our apartment complex. Suspecting that the mysterious van was occupied by a vehicle repossession team, I immediately made a U-turn, exited the premises, and went to my mother's house for the night.

Two mornings later, I received a call from my office, asking if I were available to meet and conduct business with a client, not far from my house. After jotting down the specifics, I got showered, dressed, and headed to the meeting. At first, I thought I was mistaken about where I had parked the night before. I scanned the parking lot for my car, to no avail. It was definitely missing. I came back inside, and contacted the finance company, who confirmed the vehicle had been repossessed. More frustrated than embarrassed, I had no choice but to inform my office that I would be unable to execute the task.

From the height of my success, to the lowest of my low, Dionne stood in my corner. She never gave me a bunch of lip about the tough times, as people tend to do. She followed wherever I led, unconcerned if the landing were high, or low ground. The cultivating experiences that Dionne and I shared, although absolutely hilarious on occasion, strengthened our bond, and paved the way for what potentially could have been a lifelong union. For instance, I allowed her to use my Mercedes to take her driver's license examination. While performing the fifty foot back-up exercise, she collided with a guard rail, creating a noticeable streak in the paint, from the front fender, to the rear quarter-panel. I wasn't a bit angry at her...I just laughed.

Another time, while driving the <u>same</u> vehicle, she rolled over a cement parking block at McDonalds, and knocked the entire exhaust system from the bottom of the car. Then, there was the winter evening that I used what little money I had, and purchased three bags of groceries. We walked from the supermarket to the car, and I placed the two bags I were carrying inside. Dionne, inadvertently, left the bag she was carrying beside the passenger's side door. We both got into the car, I backed out of the parking space, and mowed down the bag of food, smashing it to uselessness. These are the "growing pains" that shape a relationship; appreciating where you are today, while never forgetting the testimony of whence you come.

A successful relationship is based on many key elements. **Finances** are of <u>unquestionable</u> importance. Debt induces frustration, which injects calamity into the main artery of your involvement. Insufficient finances also evokes a poverty-stricken mentality, and diminishes the importance of recreational activities within your relationship. Taking your wife to a movie, even in the face of debt, is not a mismanagement of funds. Why? Because it could save your marriage. It is an inexpensive method of reducing tension, and breaking the monotony of work and domestic confinement. Debt is **very** constricting, and it's merciless clutch initiates the abolishment of thousands of relationships each year. Attempting to free yourself from it's grasp, is sometimes like swimming across an ocean, with an elephant tied to your ankle.

Communication is a substantially potent ingredient in relationship retention as well. I cannot so much as interact with anyone who assumes a defensive stance at the slightest hint of constructive criticism, or disagreement with their beliefs. I have my own mind, and will not be controlled by the theory of keeping the peace. Besides, dismissing concerns without proper resolution, virtually guarantees recurrence. Emotions are highly combustible. People finding themselves plagued with identical issues time and again, are very prone to display explosive behavior.

Communication is a tension reducer, and establishes livable terms. Occasionally, even after thorough discussion, you still may not **completely** see eye-to-eye. However, it affords at least an opportunity to meet somewhere in the middle. In your relationship, under **no** circumstance should the peak of your anger be allowed to escalate to physicality. Bats, hockey sticks, golf clubs, and boxing gloves are for **sports**, not <u>spouses</u>.

In the preceding paragraphs, I have spoken very generally about relationships. More specifically, I want to conclude this chapter by discussing the marital bed. Time or circumstance should never discount the sanctity of marriage. It is **the** greatest, most noble answer to the call of love, known to man. A strong marriage, although occasionally ambushed with challenge and unsettlement, produces strength, respect and unity. When adversities accost your marriage, your two only measures for survival are your <u>unwillingness</u> to disappoint God, and the <u>remembrance</u> of your marital vows.

Before marrying **anyone**, you should understand that entering a marriage, is entering a contract. As per <u>any</u> contract, it must be examined carefully, with a thorough understanding before signing, as <u>each</u> line has specific value. Further, you must recognize that breaching a contract enables your vulnerability to certain repercussions. The only avoidance of such repercussions, relies upon your ability to govern your actions by the parameters of the agreement.

October 14, 1995, is a day caged within the cells of my heart. This was the day I stood before everyone, who was <u>anyone</u> in my life, and granted Dionne the commitment of marriage. I still remember holding back the tears as she walked down the isle of the church. I remember how beautiful she was, and my confidence in knowing that if I had **never** done <u>anything</u> right previously, this would be the day of redemption. Later that evening, I carried her across the threshold of our small apartment, and we began a cohabitation of Godly approval.

From a teenager, I have always loved Atlantic City, and visited there frequently. Although initially, not even of legal age to be there, I found the atmosphere of the casinos breathtaking. Aside from the lights, action, and clanging sounds of coinage dropping from slot machines, there was a universal, casino gambler's advisory that I remember reading: <u>"Gamble WITH your head... not above it."</u> This is a very profound warning, not only for casino gaming participants, but to the high-rollers of life itself. Today, I pass this warning to you. <u>Never</u> wager more of <u>anything</u>

than you can afford to lose. I once rolled life's dice, and lost nearly everything to be loss.

Infidelity is not only a wager, but one of the costliest of all. Not only do you jeopardize your relationship, the lives of your children, family, and loved-ones become susceptible to adverse compromise. It is a selfish, unjustifiable, inexcusable act, which could potentially traumatize victims to the point of an emotional breakdown. Further, a widespread misconception is that to be caught, necessitates being fingered. Sometimes, evidence is circumstantial. Drastic deviations from established patterns, sometimes manifests signs of forthcoming calamity. The first hint of self stupidity, is the belief that **everyone else** is stupid.

Cheaters are subliminal lawyers. They argue a mental point with their own conscience, in an attempt to justify their actions. To do this successfully, they capitalize on the weaknesses of their mates--most of which were established from day one. However, since there is now a need to manufacture justification for immorality, these imperfections become intolerable. Whatever the motivation--when a man compromises the well-being of his family, thus does he compromise his own manhood.

While yet married to Dionne, I moronically allowed myself to fall deeply in love with another woman. I thought she was the ultimate--college educated, career-minded, bright, and vibrant. On the surface, I admired everything about her. She seemed amazingly ideal, and I thought for sure I had missed the boat. In actuality, I were the **captain** of a ship, who had deserted the entire crew.

There is **no** feeling, like the feeling of being in love. The intoxication of love, sensationalizes the most trivial happening. A mere stroll through the park, even if overrun with debris and derelicts, can be the most romantic encounter, as you walk hand in hand with your mate. My lover's almond, blemish-free face was so beautiful, and her easygoing personality added to her allure. She was very thoughtful, often writing me love letters, and cooking for me. She would buy me jewelry, clothing, and take me to fancy restaurants. Excluding Dionne, it was so refreshing, for once, to be involved with a female that added something to me. Many of the women in this town will not even know a man's full name, before they're rattling their cups like panhandlers.

Our initial relationship was bittersweet. Although we shared wonderful times, depressing ones came before us as well. Many nights, we would sit by the harbor together, crying **real** tears, wishing things could be different. I tried to hold it all together, but I was losing my grasp. My love-sickened state also took quite a toll on my job performance. My employer's patience wore increasingly thin with my outbreak of incompetence. Not only had I obviously lost my mind, denial prevented my acknowledgment that I was losing my family.

Back at the cave, my relationship with Dionne was taking a real whacking. The tension was so thick, you could touch it with your hand. Dionne was positive I were being unfaithful, but had nothing tangible to base her beliefs. What's more disgusting, is at the time, I honestly didn't even care. A time or two, I came really close to just telling Dionne outright about the affair. Confusingly enough, lying, deceiving, and creeping, really isn't my makeup; and, I wanted an end put to it.

I wanted the freedom to show the center of my joy, to the world. The once protective, loving, devoted Bear Man, had all but abandoned the cave, and his one true love...Dionne. All I could think of, night and day, was my mistress. Once praised for my exceptional performance as a father, my routine absenteeism and detachment left many mystified.

True love may become shadowed by anger from time to time, but will always shine through. While you may view getting someone into bed as a mark of accomplishment, your **first** priority should be to get into their heart. Without a secure seat there, your involvement is fruitless, and can be ceased at <u>**any**</u> time, without notice, given the slightest inducement from the person they wish **you** were. For this reason, involving yourself with the product of a "fresh breakup," is a very risky proposition. You can be almost assured, there is still plenty love buried beneath the rubble of contempt.

The situation at the cave was a time-bomb. My presence there decreased from thin to thinner, and what echoed from the walls of that house, was the hollow void of a once happy existence. On December 24, 1999, I deemed the living situation no longer tolerable, and suggested Dionne move out. It was actually just a psychological ploy for her to briefly experience life, without the benefit of my protective shield. Since I was certain that this would be only temporary, I didn't give much thought to what was actually happening. We were **officially** breaking up.

My ploy backfired. In the aftermath, December 23, 1999, would be the very last evening Dionne and I would share a home. Under normal circumstances, the misery of being apart from Dionne would have literally killed me. However, with a beautiful, vibrant, supportive mistress by my side, I was afforded somewhat a buffer from reality. Truth was, in my drunken stupor of infatuation, I actually convinced myself that I loved my mistress more than Dionne anyway. So, good-bye, and good riddance. Right? Keep reading.

Dionne's belongings were not even completely evacuated before I moved my lover into my home. I was excited about our new life together, and overjoyed that she no longer had to be a best kept secret. Knowing the prevalence of her insecurity, I unceasingly showered her with kindness and reassurance. I rushed home to her immediately when my shift was over, and did anything and everything I thought would make her feel welcomed. Despite all the hell and havoc to be faced outside my front door, **inside**, lived the happiest resident of suburban Maryland.

In the relationship game, remember one key factor. It is imperative to remain cognizant of the circumstances in which you initially connected with a person. Once a cheater, always a cheater? Not necessarily. Some, guided by the error of their ways, actually do aim to be better people. However, once the <u>potential</u> to cheat has been demonstrated, it will always exist.

Once all moved in, my mistress disappointed me, almost immediately. She had no maternal instinct whatsoever, and offered very marginal assistance with the girls. In fact, there was no real benefit to the cohabitation. I began to catch her in lie after lie, and her whereabouts were often unaccounted for. She wasn't particularly witty in the scheme of things, and her flaky explanations were usually an insult to my intelligence.

Knowing I had everything to lose if things went south, I routinely found myself compromising my own common sense. To see matters for what they were, meant facing that my pockets were turned inside-out. Every dime to my name had been laid on the table, the bets were sealed, and the roulette wheel of life was spinning. A loss, at this point, would be catastrophic, and potentially unrecoverable.

In the end, all I could do was standby helplessly, as the pit-boss of life declared me a loser. Mutually, it were agreed that perhaps we weren't so perfect for each other after all. I were to walk away with nothing; no girlfriend, wife, family or inner-peace. Now, with my breastplate removed, the sword of reality penetrated my heart, which bled relentlessly for Dionne.

In a sense, marriages are like houses--first you build, then you enjoy. Just as our struggle had come full circle; when finances were no longer an issue, and more energy could be devoted to enjoying one another, I bulldozed the entire struggle, to ground zero. The wager I chose to make, would prove to be the single greatest progressional setback, of my entire life.

Until this day, the emotional scars are noticeable, and I have not completely forgiven myself. I care for Dionne, and am swift to accredit her periodic shenanigans, to the mental anguish I imposed. I not only dishonored a marital vow, but a personal pledge to love, and protect her forever. Each day, I live with the pain and guilt. For years, I have tried to indemnify her with financial favors, and materialistic things.

The removal of fantasy from life, yields raw and shocking truisms. First, without history, <u>love</u> is commonly confused with <u>infatuation</u>. The "tingly sensation" you feel for someone you've known for a summer, is not even in the same ballpark with someone you have loved for fifteen years. Do not fool yourself. Denial of the truth is the initial stage of insanity.

There is a crap table in **each** of our lives; but, be warned: <u>place your bets carefully</u>. Since the dawn of time, man's inability to resist temptation has been his downfall. Compare the wagers in your life to the elegant, enchanting casinos of Atlantic City. Those marbled floors, gold trimmed fixtures, and crystal chandeliers were <u>**not**</u> paid for by the winners!

I know what you're thinking...is there any hope for reconciliation with Dionne? Trust is a precious thing--even more so than silver or gold. Once broken--although the victim may genuinely claim and desire to forgive you, the mere potential for a recurrence typically beclouds the relationship. Some choose to forgive, but not forget. As dysfunctional as this is, as aforementioned, a victim of trauma needs the liberty to recover from his/her upset, by any method they feel is the most effective. Nonetheless, when you allow the memories of victimization to tarry in your heart, residual enragement can overtake your existence at any time. This very scenario plagues

Dionne's life, resulting in periodic mood swings, and derogatory verbal outbursts.

There is no greater stride towards adulthood, than facing reality. For many, the truth is too difficult to stomach. Resultantly, their perception of life is what they wish it were, rather than what it actually is. Others suffer from what I call the "blame it on the rain syndrome." For these sufferers, any adverse happening in their lives are **always** the fault of someone else. Accountability is <u>never</u> assumed in any situation, under any circumstance.

In life, we make choices; some good, others not so clever. Although from small children, we are equipped with at least a rudimentary sense of right and wrong, we still sometimes make conscious, detrimental decisions. We have no concept of what is at stake, because we have no concept of things going bad. Sometimes, life affords second chances. Other times, your actions, or lack of same, causes you to miss the chance of a lifetime. I can only hope that Dionne forgives me, and the positive memories overshadows the negative ones in her mind, and heart. I respectfully dedicate this chapter to <u>Dionne K. Brown</u>.

Chapter 4:
Bringing Closure & Knowing What's Important

Even if completely unintentional, our words, actions, or a combination of the two, may occasionally be found hurtful or offensive by others. Although what we say may be overflowing with truth, we should never structurally engineer words for the purpose of reducing another person's self-worth. Malevolent commentary is <u>especially</u> destructive, when it derives from the mouths of people we trust. While some victims may decry your distasteful actions or tone then and there, others will quietly retreat into a deep shell of heavy-heartedness; sometimes, for years.

Technically, you are *only* accountable for an infraction, if you realize that one has occurred in the first place. However, the burden of reconciliation **immediately** lies with you, upon your knowledge that your words or deeds have had an injurious impingement on someone's life. If you choose to ignore it, you are guilty of malice. To assure a clear understanding, a **victim**, as referenced here, is a person who with no provocation, caught an unfavorable aftershock of your bad mood, bad day, or frustrations with life. If **two** people have <u>jointly</u> engaged in a noxious exchange of words, <u>neither</u> parties are a victim. They are simply two people who behaved badly.

There is a phenomenal amount of healing in a genuine apology. Although it cannot revoke the ill emotions generated by the initial contravention, it is an excellent stride to closure. Some owe their now adult children a long overdue apology, because they have clearly failed them as parents. Others must seek the forgiveness of their present or former spouse, because they allowed infidelity to infiltrate their marriage. Whatever the ghost underneath your bed--if you recognize that you have wronged someone, you owe them restitution.

As an offender, your road to redemption may be flooded with adversity. It will require substantial maturity, humility, and open-mindedness. First, it takes a **mature** person to <u>admit</u> fault, offer a sincerely apology, and make an honest effort to indemnify the victim. Second, you must **humble** yourself to the feedback of those you have offended, which may subject you to withstand criticism. Third, you must have an open mind to the victim's position, and be prepared for rejection. There is no law which suggests that your apology <u>must</u> be accepted by the victim.

The harsh reality is that sometimes, people do not desire your apology. They feel you have damaged them beyond repair, and would much prefer to simply exile you from their existence. These are the very real consequences of poor choices. You cannot instruct others how to react to, or process their emotional or psychological jolts. People have the <u>absolute</u> prerogative to process trauma, and recover in whichever way they deem effective.

Pride, stubbornness, and fear of rejection prevents many apologies. As hard-feelings continue to fester over unresolved issues, many offenders find convenience in evasion, and leave these issues without address. Victims attempting to live more fulfilled lives will sometimes voluntarily divorce themselves from the servitude of unforgiveness, hated, and animosity, with no apologetic action whatsoever, on the part of the offender. While this is the end result that many offenders hope for, it is a coward's exoneration. Many offenders, either through religious convictions or personal atonement, make sincere vows to walk as new beings.

Thousands even become ministers, planting themselves upon pulpits nationwide, delivering spiritual prescriptions for love, peace, and right-standing. Nevertheless, if the emotionally marred people from their past, who were never even given the benefit of an apology, could easily fill <u>every</u> pew in their sanctuary, those ministers should refocus, and rethink the foundation in which their message is based. Unless you are prepared and willing to accept ownership for your actions, and deploy **every** effort to restore the quality of another's life in which you compromised, the only thing *changed* about you is your clothing.

The heat of your past intensifies a thousand degrees when you assume a role of leadership or prestige. As politicians, entertainers, and even ministers go about their daily lives, there is never a video camera, or watchful eye of someone looking to generate scuttlebutt, far behind. Their lives are targeted, and laid beneath the microscope of those seeking to discount their persona. For any person of influence, a debatable past virtually assures a turbulent future. In the life of a celebrity, something as minuscule as a speeding ticket ignites a media frenzy.

Arguably, the media's unquenchable thirst for popularity and high ratings, commoves it to furnish detailed coverage of absolute hogwash. Cognizant that drama sells, they misuse the long-arm power of broadcast to intrude upon the day to day lives of public figures. If a basketball player is arrested for driving while intoxicated, what necessitates the airing of this information on every major television network, and the cover of every news publication? Who cares? Everyone does! Why? Because sex and drama has more marketability than any other storyline.

As a creative writer, I could have very easily written this book about eroticism, and sold two to three times as many copies. However, I prefer to write material that has a benefit, lasting longer than ten minutes. The overwhelming majority of everyday people would much rather view exclusive coverage of a celebrity's sex scandal, than the progress of the war in Iraq. Much of the riffraff that the five o'clock news anchors deliver to our living rooms, is not news at all. It is insignificant tidings, which should be aired on an entertainment channel.

<u>News</u>, is information that affects, or has the *potential* to affect the quality of your life or land. <u>Entertainment</u> broadcasts, on the other hand, is the sharing of intelligence which has **<u>no</u>** affect, or potential to affect your life or land, in any

way, shape, form or fashion. Acknowledge the difference.

Any human being is subject to flaw. A celebrity's fans often become so captivated by their persona and superstardom, that when the actual human being shines through, it is literally devastating. For a public figure, the heart of an admirer is easily broken. Even in temperatures topping one-hundred degrees, they are expected by their fan-base to pose for photographs, sign autographs, and submit to unofficial interviews. If they are dismissive, irritated, short, or less than friendly, regardless the reason, reporters see that this information is shared with every interested American.

Chapter 5:
Intimacy without nudity

The poetry of Valdez V. Fisher, Jr.

I Guess The River keeps Flowing

Are you being real with yourself?
Or, is the truth too hard to face?
Can "Mr. Muscles" REALLY take my place?

Do you ever think of me, although you're with him?
Do you wish I were the one wiping your sweat at the gym?
As you give him a "charity" hug, at the end of your date...
do you force yourself to believe he is your soul mate?

Does he make you smile and laugh, the way that I do?
Do you miss the way I make love to you?
Remember when I would bring you hot chocolate,
in the middle of the night?
Remember when I'd look under your bed,
to make sure you were all right?
Remember we visited the firing range,
and I taught you to shoot a gun?
Remember how I would hug you,
when you were sad and missing your son?
Remember I nicknamed you "Gypsy,"
because you were constantly walking somewhere?
Remember how I would kiss your lips,
and play with your dread-locked hair?

And now you claim to be happy without me? You're
telling people we're through?
Who are you trying to convince, "Gyp Gyp?" Is **them**,
or is it <u>YOU</u>?

But I've still got love for you--
for us, it simply did not work.
I can admit that a time or two, I acted like a jerk.
And yet, I loved you so much, making it hard to let go;
but when you constantly dwell in the past, it becomes
impossible to grow.

I wish only the best for you;
I wish you to find love, that is genuinely true.
I wish you to be real, and I wish you to be free--
but can you honestly look that man in the eye, and tell
him you don't love me?

The Crossroads

As we sat on the wooden bench, and waited for her train--
my heart was in the deepest, most undescribable pain.
Although all choked up, I refused to cry;
as I thought to myself, why must it always end with
"Good Bye?"

As evidence of a tear, slowly began to fill my eye...
with a swift wipe from my palm, I made it dry.
Who would be there to hold me? Who would comfort
me? For the attendant announced her train was
arriving, on track E.

I stood to my feet, and looked into her face--
for the short time that she stayed, she filled this empty space.
But now she had to return, to a life all her own;
and, as for me...the same as usual...sad and all alone.

I try not to think of her much. I know it will do no good.
I still hold back the tears, but I wonder if I should?
For what seems to be forever,
I have walked alone in the rain;
with open wounds that bleed for true love,
I constantly ignore the pain.
Sometimes I wonder, what is really left to gain?
Has the bitterness of a lonely heart, driven me insane?

I hope she knows I love her,
for it is now that I see;
happiness is still possible, for I felt it before she left me.

Will it ever happen?

I know I am asking a lot of you.
I know you don't know me well.
I am asking you to trust me;
and to come out of your shell.

I think I am in love with you;
I know that must sound insane.
I have visions of kissing your soft, sweet lips,
and singing to you in the rain.

Am I a hopeless romantic?
Or, am I a fool living a fantasy?
Can I really expect you to heed these words,
and share a life with me?

Your reluctant heart may be full of scars;
so, at night, as I look towards the stars---
I will wait for the moment in which you say,
"I cannot live without you another day."

Tell me something:

Is it that you don't want to love me?
Or, do you see me as all the rest?
Have I made any progress with you;
or, have I failed the test?

Is it wrong of me to miss you?
Is it wrong to want to kiss you?
Is it wrong to want to hold your hand?
Is it wrong to want to be your man?

You have built a wall I cannot penetrate.
I can never enter your heart, for you have locked the gate.
The more I beg and beg you for the key...
the faster you run away from me.

I know you've been hurt, and it's difficult to trust.
I know that men often confuse love with lust.
I know to you, it all sounds like game...
just another smooth talker, only a different name.

Each day I grab hold of the imaginary chain,
and wonder if all my efforts are in vein.
Will the padlock remain, until it is covered with rust?
And, will all my hopes and dreams crumble fruitless
into dust?

You Wonder

You wonder if I really love you?
You wonder if I'm sincere?
You wonder if my life is fulfilled, now that you're here?

They say life is short, although it can be very long.
To live a lonely, empty life, is like a sad love song.
A song that never ends...verse after depressing verse;
it's as if your entire existence, was one big curse.

When you live a life of regret...
an ocean of wrongs you can never right; as
the warm tears burn your cheeks,
while you lay in bed at night.
You wonder if you'll ever find true love again; or, if you
are fighting a battle, which you'll never win?

When you have reached your lowest low;
when you allow yourself to mentally grow...
you will finally come to know...if you really love
someone, you'd better not let go!

The pride of man is his weakness;
denial of the truth shields his ego.

So like the water of the ocean, away your soul mate
begins to flow.
Perhaps far, far away...never to be seen again; then
replays that sad, endless love song,
aforementioned, my friend.

So, you wonder if I love you?
You wonder if I'm true?
You think I want to call it quits,
and see someone new?

You are the redemption to my broken heart...
you have set my soul free.
No more sad nights, with no one to comfort me.
For the joy you have brought to my life,
and for all the things that you do...
There should be no **wonder**, why I love you.

The Reality Check

She is so beautiful...her image haunts me. When I look
to the skies, it is her face I see.
Would I gain her interest, if I wore sixty dollar cologne?
Would she be impressed with me, if I bought her a T-bone?
If I give her my number, would she call me on the phone;
or, would she rather I just leave her alone?

Would I obtain her respect, if I flashed a Platinum Card?
Would she be at all impressed, if she knew I worked hard?
Would I sweep her off her feet, if I buy a Mercedes-Benz;
or, would I just be a trophy to show her friends?

If I pretend I am rich, although I can barely eat; if I applied for store credit to put alligator shoes on my feet...would she then like me? Would she then be impressed? Could I be her man, if I were well dressed?

Or have I lost sight, of my own self worth?
Have I not made a mark on this Earth?
I may not be rich, but I am content.
I may not be stylish, but I can pay my rent.
I may not have a Mercedes, but I do not ride the bus;
there is even a small balance for me,
at the local Bank & Trust.

What if her face is just an illusion...a wonderful vision?
What if she just flies away at the first sight of trouble,
like a downtown pigeon?
What use would I have for her? Are her horizons broad
or dim? Is she actually prepared to love me,
or does she just see me as an ATM?

I think I'd rather keep walking, and leave my credit cards uncharged. It just occurred to me, that my self esteem has been garaged. Now that the door is open, I feel totally free...so if she DOES have an interest, she'd better approach ME!

"I will always love you"

As you journey through this lifetime,
people will come, and they will go.
Our lives are sometimes permanently impacted,
by the ones we come to know.

As we interact with people, it is
often plain to see...
that the bond we create,
and the memories we build,
shall last an eternity.

This is my tribute, so I must swallow my pride...
this void I carry, no longer can I hide.
So this is the time, I have set aside...
to honor those who are yet living,
and those who have died.

Although we may seem,
a whole world apart.....
you shall ALWAYS have-
a special place in my heart.

We have been separated by life,
and the change that it brings.
But I will forever love you,
and nothing can change things.

Please accept my tribute,
for what I say is true--
just as sure as this world rotates,
"I WILL ALWAYS LOVE YOU."

Please listen to me...

Do you know what love is? Do you really?

Love is an action word.
Love is unconditional.
Love is sacrifice.
Love is acceptance.
Love is consideration.
Love is forgiveness.
Now ask yourself, who do you love?

Don't wait too late to say, "I love you"

Call her today, and tell her something sweet.
Even send her some flowers; hey, that would be neat.

Compliment her hair style, and the sparkle of her eyes.
Make each day she awakens to you, yet another
wonderful surprise.

Tell her how good dinner was,
as you gently stroke her face;
tell her that no one could ever take her place.

Tell her she's beautiful, and her smile lights the earth.
See to it that she has the highest level of self-worth.

For somewhere lurking is some interceptor,
who will replace you as her king.
He will love her, and protect her, and give her his ring.

I am speaking from example, so whatever you do,
please don't wait too late to say, "I love you."

The beauty of a girl

The glistening of a diamond,
or the radiance of the sun;
the blue of a still water, or the sweetness of a bun.
The smell of a new pine tree,
planted by a lake.
Or, the purity of a perfectly white snowflake.
The stars in the sky, or all the money in this world--
can **never** compare, to the beauty of a girl.

"You"

The confession of a confused heart:

Could she be the one; or, should I turn and walk away?
Without her, how shall I face another day?

My love...

As I sat at the breakfast table of the restaurant this
morning, all I could think of was you.

As I laid my head down to rest last night, all I could
think of was you.

When I have my fondest, most exotic thoughts, I think
only of you.

I go out of my way to be wherever you are. I am so
ready to hold you close to me, and protect you, and

love you, and erase your hurt, and your pain, and your disappointment.

To kiss your lips, I would forfeit the beauty of the moon, and the stars, and the ocean, and the sea; the birds of the sky, and the pedals of the roses.

If only you knew the things I would do for "**You.**"

"How Can This Be"

New romance is the candle that lights the dimmest corner of a shattered heart:

If I had no money, and had to ride the bus;
if my checking account was overdrawn, and the bank put up a fuss--
if I had an eviction notice, for failure to pay rent; and, every employer appeared to be ignoring the resume I've sent...
I would still be as happy, as a child on Christmas Day--
for the way you have touched my heart, my love, words cannot say.
The kiss of your thin lips, and your tender embrace--
the sparkle of your eyes, and your beautiful face;
the way that you smile, and the way that you talk--
the way that you move, and the way that you walk...
makes me want to sail away with you, across a beautiful sea;
to give you my seed, and to make you fall in love with me.
Sometimes at night, while on bent knee, I look to the skies and whisper:
How Can This Be?

Anything worth having is worth waiting for

As she walked down the city street...
I knew this was one girl, I just had to meet.
She had the thickest thighs, yet somewhat petite...
and looked irresistable from her head, to her feet.

I pulled along side her, and politely said, "Hello."
Then, I asked where she were about to go.

While looking into her hazel eyes--
she asked a question, to my surprise.
"Do you ever think of your demise?"
And I immediately shifted my attention from her thighs.

What ever do you mean, my pretty girl?
Do I ever think of leaving this world?
Yes, all the time, I would have to say;
but, what about you? What are WE doing today?

Then she smiled at me, with her perfect skin tone...
as I asked for the number to her telephone.
Trying not to be shallow was really a test;
but I was determined to prove I were different from the rest.

A few nights later, while laying across her bed...
on her soft, flat stomach, I planted my head.
I soon fell asleep as she gently stroked my cheek;
I could tell she loved me...after just one week.

I awakened to find it very late;
I could have had my way that night, but I decided to wait.
So, careful not to awaken her, I headed for the door--
thinking to myself, next time, for sure!
Sleep well, my lady.

The Hopeless Romantic

When morning comes, and the night has passed--
when I have connected with your soul, at last.When the
light of the sun shows your half-awake smile,
and we wonder if we've created a child.

As I feed you breakfast in our bed--
when I hold you gently, and rub your precious head.
As I kiss you softly on your sweet thin lips;
while teasing you by nibbling around your hips.
I feel I am the luckiest man alive--
could the girl I have been waiting for, finally have arrived?
You make me feel like a millionaire, although I am not rich.
You make me want to sing to you, although I'd be off pitch.
You make me want to fly away with you,
across the clear blue sky;
I am dangerously in love with you...this, I cannot deny.
I now know why they say the best things in life are free...
my darling, would you please spend the rest of your life
with me?

"The Pain I Feel"

To Dionne:

When I were very young, and yet in junior high school--
I met a girl, who I thought was so cool.

We grew very close, and as it came to be...
the day surely came, when she marrird me.

We started very poor, barely a dime to our names;
and, soon a little bundle of joy came.

I had searched for work, without any avail;
I felt that I were destined to fail.

I dressed my best, for the employers to see;
yet, one by one, they rejected me.

All I had was my wife, who was good to me--
she was full of support, and loyalty.

There were times I'd leave home, with less than a buck--
trying to locate work, and hoping for good luck.

Then before very long, I received some good news;
I was made a job offer, I could not refuse.

I found a career, that took great care of me;
now, I could be the man that I was supposed to be.

My wife and I became examples to our friends--
I even went out, and bought us a Benz.

But with success, it appears, came lots of trouble;
after five years of marriage, it destroyed our love bubble.

Instead of giving my new employer my life,
I should have spent more time loving my wife.

We were so much closer, when our pockets were low.
But now, I was constantly on the go.

Success can make you very unappreciative too;
suddenly, the simple things in life aren't good enough
for you.

I would ALWAYS have a wife; oh so I THOUGHT;
but, we are soon headed downtown, for divorce court.

We eliminated the principals, which helped us begin.
We left the door wide open, for infidelity to come in.

We turned a cold back, to one another--
at times, we didn't even seem to love each other.

So, how sad this poem, but I tell you it's true.
I hope my writing teaches you;
material things are no big deal...
I'd trade it all to disintegrate
"THE PAIN I FEEL"

"Thank You"

Although I am an adult,
I often look back--
at all of the discipline I would lack;
if it had not been for the love and care,
of those who helped raise me, and those who were there.

To those who taught me to sweep a floor,
and those who taught me to "lock the door."
To those who said, "Boy, wash your face;"
and taught me that school, was the place!

To those who told me to watch for cars,
and those who said to reach for the stars.
To those who taught me, Christ is king--
and love and blessings shall he bring.

To those who taught me to show others love,
and those who have passed on, and now live above...

Please believe that what I say is true,
from the bottom of my heart, I say:

Thank you.

"Walk Upright"

Sometimes I observe my children,
watching them laugh and play.
I allow them to be kids;
yet, I teach them to obey.

We adults sometimes forget,
that we must devise a plan;
for the lives of our children,
are in the palm of our hand.

When a child is born into this world,
he does not know to hate.
He does not know black from white,
or what it means to segregate.

So we must be positive influences,
for our impressionable ones to mimic.
So sad that youthful crime and pregnancy,
has become an epidemic.

To be an effective mentor,
is for what I must fight.
This is why my daily struggle, is to WALK UPRIGHT.

To my Mother:

You are my sunshine, my only sunshine-
you make my happy, when skies are gray.
You will NEVER know, just how much I love you...
don't ever take my sunshine away.
I love you...I would leave this world for you at <u>ANY</u> time.

The Consequence

I loved her immediately,
and didn't even know her real name.
We met on the Internet, where anonymity is the game.

There was something about her,
that made me want to know more.
Her text was psychotic, but it added to her allure.
Her face was beautiful, and as smooth as sand;
but, from what I could gather, she had a man.

Many people online, wished her banished;
they wanted her abrasive text vanished.
But, I wasn't a part of the hate group;
no, not me.
Her demented come-across, aroused my curiosity.

Each time she would call, I would silently smile;
this girl was absolutely nuts, but I loved her style.
I waited patiently, for the "psycho act" to wear thin;
but, her conversation never deviated much, from
the chat room we met in.

And yet, I felt a comfort zone;
we would spend hours on the telephone.
She gave hints of normality, here and there;
but to be honest, I really did not care.

As we began to talk more and more,
I learned that she had a sweet, soft core.
I confided in her, as she listened to me;
I was falling in love with her; how could this be?

I would stare into her pictures,
and long to hold her tight.
I wished we could share a bed at night.

I wanted to make love to her;
and, she voiced a desire too.
So I journeyed to see her, without
further ado.

I held her close to me,
and never wanted to let go.
I genuinely loved her, and I wanted her to know.

I kissed her lips, and looked into her eyes;
but, next, I was in for a BIG surprise.
"We can't sleep together," she said to me.
"I've never cheated before; it's only a fantasy."

I was not at all angry,
but just a little sad.
I guess that's what happens, when you plot to do bad.
I felt really lonely, when she had to go;
I wondered where all this would lead me,
and now I know.

Chapter 6:
"Valdezinary"

Favorite words of the author:

1. <u>**Aforementioned**</u>: : mentioned previously

2 <u>**Befuddle**</u>: **1 :** to muddle or stupefy with or as if with drink **2 :** <u>CONFUSE</u>, <u>PERPLEX</u>

3. <u>**Calamity**</u>: **1 :** a state of deep distress or misery caused by major misfortune or loss **2 :** an extraordinarily grave event marked by great loss and lasting distress and affliction

4. <u>**Forthcoming**</u>: **1 :** being about to appear or to be produced or made available <the *forthcoming* holidays> <your *forthcoming* novel> **2 a:** <u>RESPONSIVE</u>, <u>OUTGOING</u> <a *forthcoming* and courteous man> **b:** characterized by openness, candidness, and forthrightness

5. <u>**Gratuitous**</u>: **1 a :** given unearned or without recompense **b :** not involving a return benefit, compensation, or consideration **c :** costing nothing : <u>FREE</u> **2 :** not called for by the circumstances : <u>UNWARRANTED</u>

6. **Malevolent**: 1 : having, showing, or arising from intense often vicious ill will, spite, or hatred 2 : productive of harm or evil-ma·lev·o·lent·ly *adverb*

7. **Regalia**: 1 : royal rights or prerogatives 2 a : the emblems, symbols, or paraphernalia indicative of royalty b: decorations or insignia indicative of an office or membership 3 : special dress; *especially:* FINERY

8. **Retrospect**: 1 : *archaic* : reference to or regard of a precedent or authority 2 : a review of or meditation on past events-**in retrospect** : in considering the past or a past event

9. **Rudimentary**: 1 : consisting in first principles : FUNDAMENTAL <had only a *rudimentary* formal education 2 : of a primitive kind <the equipment of these past empire-builders was *rudimentary* 3 : very imperfectly developed or represented only by a vestige <the *rudimentary* tail of a hyrax>

10. **Wherewithal**: : MEANS, RESOURCES; *specifically:* MONEY <didn't have the *wherewithal* for an expensive dinner>

Chapter 7:
Memories Captured

Rosalind

Sammie

Dionne

Dionne   Sammie   Rosalind

Valdez

Chapter 8:
Bloopers from the past

When I were in the second grade, Ms. Diane Christopher, my teacher, assigned each of her students to write a poem, and share it with the class. Along with the assignment, was a due date of approximately one week. As usual, I waited until the last minute to get started, then made a frantic attempt to throw something together, on the morning it were due. I jotted down a few lines, and balled up the paper in frustration, realizing it were not my best work.

Finally, remembering that my mom wrote poetry too, I went into her scrap book and removed one, without even reading it. I'm pretty clever, I remember thinking to myself. When it were my turn to share, I removed the poem from my book bag with confidence. After waiting patiently for the **full** attention of my classmates and teacher, I began to read to them an erotic poem, written to my mother's boyfriend!

In 1994, while working at a local bookstore, a cute, short, Caucasian lady walked in, and darted to the paperback section. After making her selection, "Lasher," by **Anne Rice**, she advanced towards the front sales counter. Before handing me the book to be rung up, she took notice of a heavy, hard bound pictorial on Maryland's Eastern Shore. She picked it up, thumbed through a few pages, and almost dropped it. It retailed for forty-five dollars; and, had it fallen, the corners would have bent, and I would have had to discount the book for future sale. After asking her to please be careful, she apologized, and promptly returned the book to the shelf. Next, I facetiously remarked that she looked an awful lot like that "terminator lady." "You mean, Linda Hamilton," she asked? "Yes, I replied." She said, "Well, that's me!"

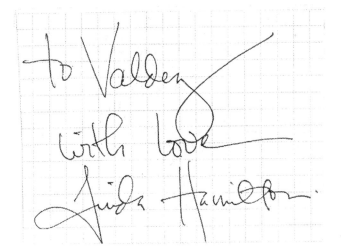

Chapter 9:
The patience in acquiring a celebrity's foreword

Actual Emails from Lance Warlock
Halloween II

Valdez -

You are to kind!
Glad to hear things are rollin along. I love to hear when people are productive doing what they love to do. Right now, we are preparing to launch the Radio Mechanics push to the world. As soon as the copies are made to sell on our site, we are there! Right now we've sent out a few to festivals and some for reviews.
We are getting a responses!

Keep up the good work! There are rewards from all of this! You will be getting a copy of RM for yourself! We are always on the look out for more projects to produce. Writing music is the first passion, but there is nothing like putting together something that you created from nothing! Like writing a book!

Take care my friend!

-Lance

Valdez -

Very nice looking! You sure you want my name on the cover? If so, OK. But
I think it's great that you are planning your attack for when it's released! That's a very important step in the whole process. Way to go!

Keep me up to date with your progress! Congratulations!!

-Lance

Valdez -

Glad to here you approve! How is everything coming at this point? I couldn't imagine being able to write Ik that. Everybody has their thing they do well I suppose! Keep me up to speed with your progress! I wish you great luck!

Talk to you soon!
-Lance

Valdez -

I have not changed my mind at all. I just can't belive how busy things are! Which is good, but very tiring! This just came out, http://www. halloweenseries.com/hqlloweenpQga   seem: fitting considering the time of year! How's everything on your end?

Have a great Halloween weekend!!

Talk to you soon!

-Lance

Valdez -

What a compliment! I've never done anything like that before. If you were to tell me what all you would want in a foreward, then I would give it my best shot! If you feel that I would be a "good" contribution, then I would give it a shot.

Thank you for the offer!

Keep me posted!

-Lance

Valdez -

Is there a way you can give me a deadline for this? That would help me in this process! I'll send you an email copy first for your approval! Then I can send hard copies. Sound good?

Let me know!

Thanks!

-Lance

Valdez -

Sounds excellent! Keep making it happen! That's what it is all about! In case we miss each other, have a great Christmas!!!

Talk to you soon!
-Lance

Valdez -
Scary! When would you need this by? My wife is a teacher, so she can proof read and help me get it sounding good!! Are you really sure that you want me to do this??? Way to cool! Sounds like things are rolling for you!

Let me know, and I'll get started!

-Lance

Valdez -

Sorry I've been out of toch for sometime. It has been very busy! As a result of that, I have not completed the forward yet! Is this OK? Can I have through the weekend? Please? Let me know on this.

As for the trailer, yes we did the music. My music partner wrote the story and co-directed the short. It's being edited as we speak. From there we will get it onto festivals and conventions. The thing that makes us the most happy is that we just did it! Just like your book! You just did it! Great accomplishment!

Talk to you soon!
-Lance

Valdez -

Hey there! I just wanted you to know that this weekend I'm going to sit down and read what all you have sent me, and start on the forward! Good for you on making something happen for yourself! That's the only way to do it! You're off to a great start!

Have a great weekend!

-Lance

You RULE!!! I was sending you one for free! Nice to support what we do!

How's everything coming?

-Lance

----- Original Message---
From: VALDEZVFiSHER@aoi.com
Dear Lance:

Just ordered my copy of Radio Mechanics. Can't wait to see it. :-)

Printed in the United States
63248LVS00008B/10-21